FOREWORD

Welcome to this 11+ Mathematics Workbook by TM Books.

This book has been compiled after much consideration of the requirements to pass the 11+ examinations and provides a good foundation of mathematics for all students prior to entering secondary school.

Education of children is understandably a cause very close to our hearts, and we truly believe that all children deserve a good quality education, giving them the best possible chance to excel at their maximum potential.

We therefore have pledged to donate at least 10% of our profits from the sale of TM Books towards the education of children from deprived areas across the world. We hope you support us in providing for this extremely worthy cause.

This book is intended for ages 9 to 12 and is specially designed to cover the most common topics covered in the 11+ entrance examinations. This book spans 50 different topics with over 2000 practice questions for your child to do, along with answers at the back of the workbook.

THE AIMS OF THE BOOK INCLUDE:
- Increasing awareness of the different topics
- Highlighting strengths and weaknesses in the core topics
- Increasing confidence
- Increasing speed and efficiency when tackling questions
- Giving lots of opportunity for PRACTICE, PRACTICE and PRACTICE!

There is a Practice Makes Perfect Index located on the bottom right corner of each set of questions, helping to track your score and progress throughout.

It is best to start the book from the beginning to help build your child's self-esteem and to work systematically. Working out is ESSENTIAL where appropriate and it is important to remind your child to check their work carefully after completing each topic. This helps promote good habits that can easily be replicated in an examination setting.

We recommend that each topic page is marked by a responsible adult, and mistakes are addressed straight away, helping to further your child's understanding and ensuring clarity.

We really hope you use this book effectively and your child enjoys working through the different types of questions. Please let us know if you have any feedback or comments at info@tmtuition.com.

CONTENTS

1.	Addition	6
2.	Subtraction	7
3.	Multiplication	8
4.	Division	9
5.	Multiplication 10/100/1000/10000	11
6.	Division 10/100/1000/10000	12
7.	Prime, Square and Cube numbers	13
8.	Lowest Common Multiple & Highest Common Factor	14
9.	Averages	15
10.	Ratios	16
11.	Proportion	22
12.	Fractions, Decimals & Percentages	26
13.	Fractions	27
14.	Percentages	39
15.	Decimals	46
16.	Decimal Points	50
17.	Significant Figures	51
18.	Standard Form	52
19.	BIDMAS	53
20.	Negative Numbers	55
21.	Algebra	58
22.	Area & Perimeter	72
23.	Area of Compound Shapes	74
24.	Circles	75
25.	Cuboids	76

26.	**Cylinders**	77
27.	**Angles**	78
28.	**3D Shapes**	81
29.	**Probability**	82
30.	**Coding**	88
31.	**Maps**	90
32.	**Metric Units**	94
33.	**Imperial Units**	96
34.	**Currency Conversion**	98
35.	**Estimation**	100
36.	**Sequences**	101
37.	**Clocks**	104
38.	**Coordinates**	110
39.	**Problem Solving**	112
40.	**Bar Charts**	115
41.	**Pie Charts**	116
42.	**Train Timetable**	118
43.	**Frequency Table**	120
44.	**Line Symmetry**	122
45.	**Rotational Symmetry**	123
46.	**Speed, Distance, Time**	124
Answers		126

CHAPTER 1
ADDITION

Work out the following questions.

1. 23 + 35 =58
2. 36 + 43
3. 56 + 64
4. 87 + 36
5. 66 + 73
6. 89 + 33
7. 95 + 54
8. 67 + 88
9. 64 + 83
10. 24 + 83
11. 195 + 254
12. 267 + 338
13. 185 + 524
14. 167 + 198
15. 189 + 212
16. 1095 + 8034
17. 2167 + 3038
18. 1850 + 4524
19. 1687 + 1998
20. 1089 + 2102
21. 23456 + 34567
22. 34234 + 98798
23. 45674 + 78787
24. 98765 + 87435
25. 54643 + 23876

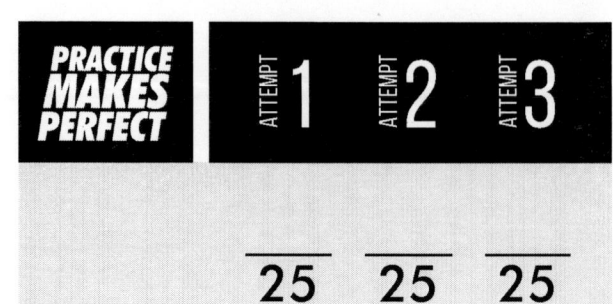

CHAPTER 2
SUBTRACTION

Work out the following questions.

1. 53 - 35
2. 96 - 43
3. 56 - 14
4. 83 - 36
5. 26 - 13
6. 99 - 35
7. 95 - 54
8. 67 - 18
9. 24 - 11
10. 84 - 23
11. 595 - 254
12. 467 - 338
13. 785 - 224
14. 867 - 198
15. 689 - 218
16. 9095 - 8034
17. 6167 - 3138
18. 8850 - 4224
19. 5687 - 1998
20. 2989 - 2002
21. 73456 - 30567
22. 84234 - 28798
23. 95674 - 71287
24. 87654 - 56787
25. 64356 - 26474

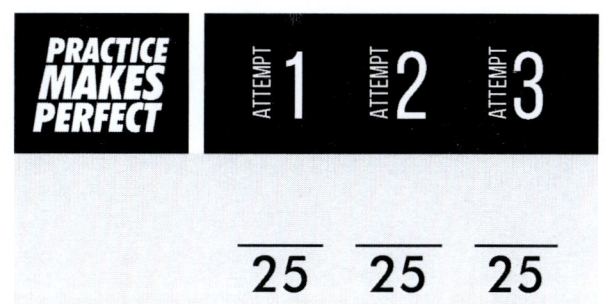

CHAPTER 3
MULTIPLICATION

Work out the following questions.

1. 5 x 6
2. 4 x 8
3. 7 x 9
4. 8 x 6
5. 9 x 5
6. 8 x 13
7. 11 x 4
8. 12 x 5
9. 13 x 6
10. 14 x 7
11. 15 x 8
12. 16 x 10
13. 11 x 11
14. 12 x 13
15. 13 x 14
16. 15 x 16
17. 18 x 17
18. 23 x 25
19. 26 x 28
20. 27 x 30
21. 29 x 35
22. 30 x 36
23. 41 x 43
24. 29 x 47
25. 76 x 98

PRACTICE MAKES PERFECT

ATTEMPT 1	ATTEMPT 2	ATTEMPT 3
/25	/25	/25

CHAPTER 4
DIVISION

Work out the following questions.

1. 10 ÷ 5
2. 20 ÷ 4
3. 30 ÷ 6
4. 40 ÷ 8
5. 49 ÷ 7
6. 30 ÷ 15
7. 45 ÷ 3
8. 121 ÷ 11
9. 144 ÷ 12
10. 169 ÷ 13
11. 225 ÷ 15
12. 100 ÷ 4
13. 200 ÷ 20
14. 250 ÷ 25
15. 190 ÷ 2
16. 186 ÷ 6
17. 306 ÷ 3
18. 248 ÷ 4
19. 129 ÷ 3
20. 147 ÷ 7
21. 225 ÷ 9
22. 195 ÷ 4
23. 126 ÷ 8
24. 122 ÷ 2
25. 2045 ÷ 5

CHAPTER 4
DIVISION
CONTINUED

Use long division to work out the following questions.

1. 4220 ÷ 4
2. 168 ÷ 7
3. 755 ÷ 5
4. 9800 ÷ 10
5. 561 ÷ 3
6. 888 ÷ 8
7. 4848 ÷ 2
8. 744 ÷ 12
9. 2624 ÷ 4
10. 1331 ÷ 11
11. 3672 ÷ 6
12. 1476 ÷ 9
13. 56 ÷ 4
14. 6251 ÷ 7

15. 1215 ÷ 5
16. 7840 ÷ 10
17. 7812 ÷ 3
18. 1056 ÷ 8
19. 78412 ÷ 2
20. 1440 ÷ 12
21. 5244 ÷ 4
22. 5412 ÷ 11
23. 102 ÷ 6
24. 1064 ÷ 5
25. 5432 ÷ 3

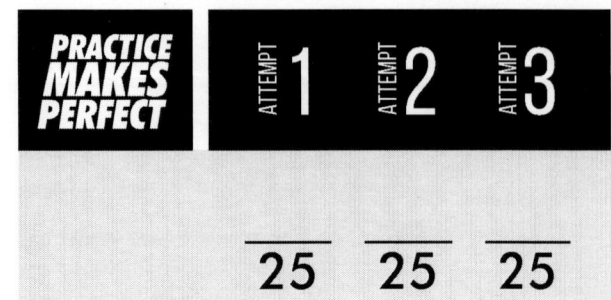

CHAPTER 5
MULTIPLICATION
10/100/1000/10000

Work out the following questions.

1. 5 x 10
2. 7 x 100
3. 8 x 1000
4. 2 x 10000
5. 0.4 x 10
6. 0.6 x 100
7. 0.9 x 1000
8. 0.7 x 10000
9. 14 x 10
10. 18 x 100
11. 29 x 1000
12. 45 x 10000
13. 0.05 x 10
14. 0.09 x 100
15. 0.06 x 1000
16. 0.23 x 10000
17. 101 x 10
18. 1234 x 100
19. 12389 x 1000
20. 98790 x 10000
21. 10.3 x 100
22. 1.05 x 1000
23. 230.35 x 10000
24. 353 x 100
25. 0.2345 x 1000

CHAPTER 6
DIVISION
10/100/1000/10000

Work out the following questions.

1. 1 ÷ 10
2. 2 ÷ 100
3. 5 ÷ 1000
4. 6 ÷ 10000
5. 0.3 ÷ 10
6. 0.4 ÷ 100
7. 0.7 ÷ 1000
8. 0.9 ÷ 10000
9. 12 ÷ 10
10. 15 ÷ 100
11. 52 ÷ 1000
12. 234 ÷ 10000
13. 0.03 ÷ 10
14. 0.06 ÷ 100
15. 0.008 ÷ 1000
16. 0.009 ÷ 10000
17. 1.03 ÷ 10
18. 1.06 ÷ 100
19. 10.009 ÷ 1000
20. 120.09 ÷ 10000
21. 1234 ÷ 100
22. 23456 ÷ 1000
23. 543200 ÷ 10000
24. 435 ÷ 1000
25. 543 ÷ 100

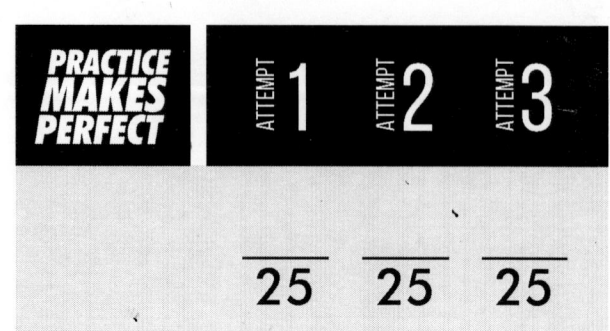

CHAPTER 7

PRIME, SQUARE AND CUBE NUMBERS

Look at the numbers below. Circle the prime numbers, underline the square numbers, and box the cube numbers.

1	②	③	4	⑤	6	⑦	8	9	10
⑪	12	⑬	14	15	16	⑰	18	⑲	20
21	22	㉓	24	25	26	27	28	㉙	30
㉛	32	33	34	35	36	㊲	38	39	40
㊶	42	㊸	44	45	46	㊼	48	49	50
51	52	㊼	54	55	56	57	58	㊾	60
㊿	62	63	64	65	66	㊿	68	69	70
㊀	72	㊂	74	75	76	77	78	㊃	80
81	82	㊄	84	85	86	87	88	㊅	90
91	92	93	94	95	96	㊆	98	99	100
⑩⑴	102	⑴⓪③	104	105	106	⑴⓪⑦	108	⑴⓪⑨	110
111	112	⑴⑴③	114	115	116	117	118	119	120
121	122	123	124	125	126	⑴②⑦	128	129	130
⑴③⑴	132	133	134	135	136	⑴③⑦	138	⑴③⑨	140

Hint: There are 5 cube numbers, 11 square numbers, 34 prime numbers

CHAPTER 8
LOWEST COMMON MULTIPLE & HIGHEST COMMON FACTOR

Work out the Lowest Common Multiple (a) and Highest Common Factor (b) for the following questions.

1. 5, 10
2. 4, 10
3. 3, 12
4. 6, 15
5. 6, 20
6. 9, 18
7. 10, 25
8. 10, 15
9. 10, 20
10. 9, 27
11. 20, 24
12. 18, 24
13. 14, 21
14. 7, 28
15. 20, 30
16. 12, 15
17. 16, 30
18. 18, 30
19. 25, 30
20. 40, 50
21. 30, 50
22. 50, 100
23. 150, 200
24. 14, 20
25. 25, 50

CHAPTER 9
AVERAGES

Work out the Mean (a), Mode (b), Median (c) and Range (d) for the following questions.

1. 5, 4, 3, 4
2. 2, 2, 3, 4, 9
3. 2, 4, 6, 6, 12
4. 2, 6, 7, 9, 6
5. 1, 11, 2, 10, 6, 6
6. 5, 5, 5, 5, 5
7. 5, 7, 9, 10, 10, 10, 19
8. 12, 12, 12, 10, 14
9. 8, 14, 10, 10, 16, 2, 10
10. 20, 30, 40, 50, 50, 50,
11. -2, -2, 4, 4, 4
12. -1, -3, -2, -2, -4
13. -5, -4, -3, 3, 3, 6,
14. -10, -12, -12, -12, -4
15. 1, 11, 21, 31, 11
16. 10, 11, 12, 13, 14, 15, 16, 17, 12, 20
17. 6, 5, 4, 3, 6, 6
18. 3, 2, 1, 1, 7, 7, 7,
19. 5, 3, 9, 5, 8
20. 2, 2, 6, 10
21. -1, -2, -3, -3, -3, -6
22. -1, -9, -11, -11, -8
23. 10, 10, 10, 10, 10, 10
24. 5, 7, 8, 8, 12
25. 1, 2, 2, 2, 3

CHAPTER 10

RATIOS

Simplify the following ratios.

1. 10:15
2. 20:30
3. 10:12
4. 4:8
5. 6:10
6. 9:15
7. 5:15
8. 20:25
9. 3:9
10. 6:24
11. 35:50
12. 2:6
13. 3:12
14. 11:33
15. 12:48
16. 10:36
17. 15:45
18. 40:50
19. 30:100
20. 50:100
21. 55:110
22. 30:40
23. 1000:5000
24. 80:1000
25. 120:360

PRACTICE MAKES PERFECT	ATTEMPT 1	ATTEMPT 2	ATTEMPT 3
	___ / 25	___ / 25	___ / 25

CHAPTER 10
RATIOS
CONTINUED

Work out the following questions.

1. Share £10 in the ratio 1:4
2. Share £10 in the ratio 1:9
3. Share £20 in the ratio 2:3
4. Share £30 in the ratio 2:1
5. Share £30 in the ratio 2:3
6. Share £50 in the ratio 1:4
7. Share £25 in the ratio 2:3
8. Share £18 in the ratio 1:8
9. Share £100 in the ratio 2:3
10. Share £150 in the ratio 3:7
11. Share £120 in the ratio 2:1
12. Share £120 in the ratio 1:3
13. Share £160 in the ratio 1:4
14. Share £10 in the ratio 2:8
15. Share £20 in the ratio 5:20
16. Share £30 in the ratio 3:12
17. Share £50 in the ratio 10:15
18. Share £100 in the ratio 10:40
19. Share £80 in the ratio 2:6
20. Share £1000 in the ratio 10:40
21. Share £2000 in the ratio 9:11
22. Share £5000 in the ratio 50:200
23. Share £300 in the ratio 5:25
24. Share £100 in the ratio 2:3
25. Share £35 in the ratio 1:4

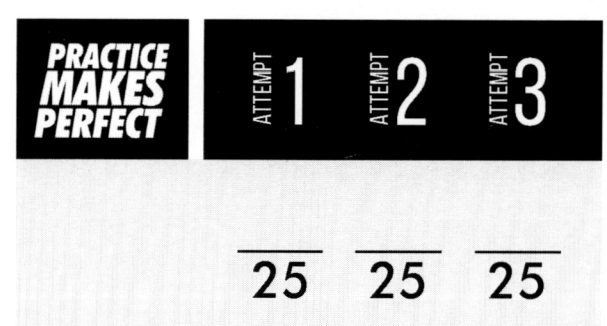

CHAPTER 10
RATIOS
CONTINUED

Work out the following questions.

1. Share £30 so that T gets double V.

2. Share £60 so that T gets double V.

3. Share £90 so that T gets double V.

4. Share £180 so that T gets double V

5. Share £3600 so that T gets double V.

6. Share £300 so that T gets half as much of V.

7. Share £600 so that T gets half as much of V.

8. Share £1200 so that T gets half as much of V.

9. Share £50 so that T gets £10 more than V.

10. Share £100 so that T gets £20 more than V.

11. Share £200 so that T gets £40 more than V.

12. Share £500 so that T gets £100 more than V.

13. Share £800 so that T gets £200 more than V.

14. Share £7 so that T gets double P, who gets double S.

15. Share £70 so that T gets double P, who gets double S.

16. Share £210 so that T gets double P, who gets double S.

17. Share £700 so that T gets double P, who gets double S.

18. Share £1400 so that T gets double P, who gets double S.

19. Share £120 so that T gets treble P, who gets half as much as S.

20. Share £240 so that T gets treble P, who gets half as much as S.

21. Share £480 so that T gets treble P, who gets half as much as S.

22. Share £960 so that T gets treble P, who gets half as much as S.

23. Share £96 so that T gets treble P, who gets half as much as S.

24. Share £300 so that T gets double P, who gets half as much as H.

25. Share £600 so that T gets double P, who gets half as much as H.

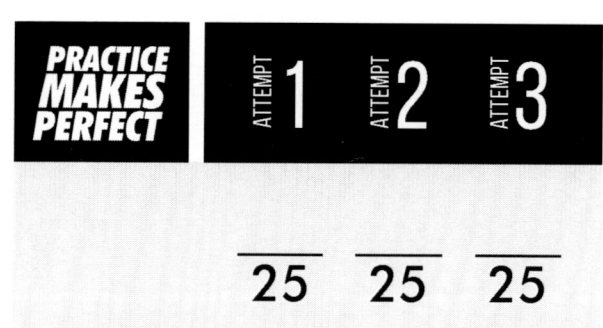

CHAPTER 10
RATIOS
CONTINUED

Work out the following questions.

1. In a class there are girls and boys in the ratio 2:1 respectively. If there are 12 girls:
   a. How many boys are there?
   b. How many children in the class?

2. In a class there are girls and boys in the ratio 3:2 respectively. If there are 15 girls:
   a. How many boys are there?
   b. How many children in the class?

3. In a class there are girls and boys in the ratio 4:3 respectively. If there are 16 girls:
   a. How many boys are there?
   b. How many children in the class?

4. In a class there are girls and boys in the ratio 5:4 respectively. If there are 10 girls:
   a. How many boys are there?
   b. How many children in the class?

5. In a class there are girls and boys in the ratio 3:1 respectively. If there are 18 girls:
   a. How many boys are there?
   b. How many children in the class?

6. In a school there are teachers, boys and girls in the ratio 1:15:20 respectively. If there are 10 teachers:
   a. How many boys are there in the school?
   b. How many girls are there in the school?
   c. How many people in total are there in the school?

7. In a school there are teachers, boys and girls in the ratio 2:20:30 respectively. If there are 20 teachers:
   a. How many boys are there in the school?
   b. How many girls are there in the school?
   c. How many people in total are there in the school?

8. In a school there are teachers, boys and girls in the ratio 5:30:35 respectively. If there are 600 boys:
   a. How many teachers are there in the school?
   b. How many girls are there in the school?
   c. How many people in total are there in the school?

9. A student has a collection of pens, pencils and rulers in his pencil case in the ratio 4:5:1. If there are 8 pens:
   a. How many pencils are there?
   b. How many rulers are there?
   c. How many items in total are there in the pencil case?

10. A student has a collection of pens, pencils and rulers in his pencil case in the ratio 5:6:4. If there are 20 rulers:
    a. How many pencils are there?
    b. How many pens are there?
    c. How many items in total are there in the pencil case?

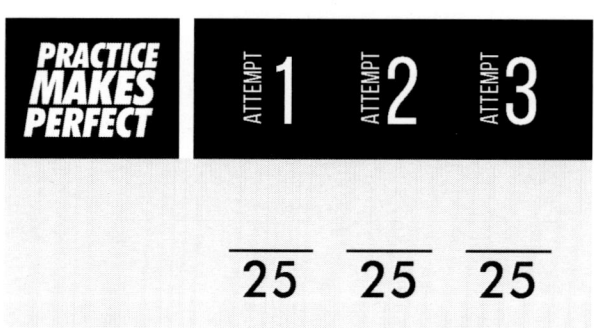

CHAPTER 11
PROPORTION

Work out the following questions.

1. If 5 calculators cost £10, what is the cost of 8 calculators?

2. If 5 calculators cost £15, what is the cost of 20 calculators?

3. If 5 calculators cost £100, what is the cost of 31 calculators?

4. John drove 100 miles with 20 litres of petrol. How many miles can he drive with 50 litres of petrol?

5. Mark drove 80 miles with 20 litres of petrol. How many miles can he drive with 120 litres of petrol?

6. Steve drove 40miles with 10 litres of petrol. How many miles can he drive with 80 litres of petrol?

7. 10 car park tickets cost £80, what is the cost of 25 car park tickets?

8. 12 car park tickets cost £100, what is the cost of 30 car park tickets?

9. 50 car park tickets cost £80, what is the cost of 70 car park tickets?

10. 12 pens cost £6, what is the cost of 100 pens?

11. 24 pens cost £6, what is the cost of 72 pens?

12. 36 pens cost £12, what is the cost of of 18 pens?

13. 100 pens cost £10, what is the cost of of 20 pens?

14. 12 apples cost £4.80. What is the cost of 20 apples?

15. 20 apples cost £12.20. What is the cost of 60 apples?

16. 100 apples cost £9.80. What is the cost of 20 apples?

17. Half a dozen of eggs cost £1.20. What is the cost of 36 eggs?

18. A dozen of eggs cost £6. What is the cost of 2 eggs?

19. A car travels 100 miles in 3 hours. How far will it have travelled in 6 hours?

20. It takes 4 hours to build a toy car. How many hours will it take to build 100 toy cars?

21. 5 miles is equivalent to 8 kilometres. How many kilometres is 500 miles equivalent to?

22. 5 miles is equivalent to 8 kilometres. How many kilometres is 100 miles equivalent to?

23. 5 miles is equivalent to 8 kilometres. How many kilometres is 200 miles equivalent to?

24. A cyclist travels 20 kilometres in 2 and a half hours. How far will the cyclist have travelled in 10 hours?

25. A cyclist travels 40 kilometres in 2 hours. How far will the cyclist have travelled in 12 hours?

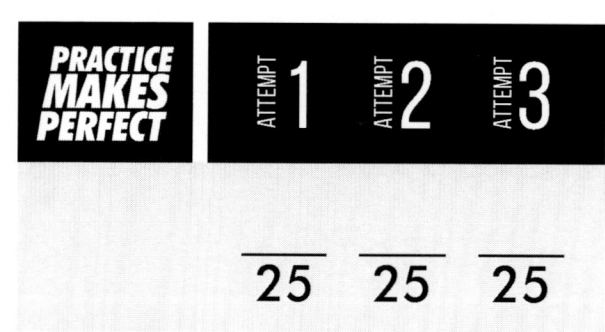

CHAPTER 11
PROPORTION
CONTINUED

Work out the following questions.

1. It takes 2 builders 6 days to fit tiles on the bathroom walls. How long would it take 4 builders to fit the tiles on the wall?

2. If 3 farmers are needed to water an acre of field within 9 days, how long would it take for 9 farmers to water the same acre of field?

3. A total of 4 pumps are required to fill the school swimming pool in 4 hours. How long would it take 2 pumps to fill the pool?

4. If it takes 2 people 5 hours to paint the bedroom completely, how long would it take 1 person to paint the same bedroom completely?

5. To cook a three-course meal for a full house of customers, it takes 4 chefs a total of 6 hours preparation. How long would it take 12 chefs to prepare a three-course meal for a full house of customers?

6. A team of 3 people are required in order to distribute flyers to all the houses in Buckinghamshire within 2 days. How many days would it take for 1 person to distribute all the flyers?

7. In order to build a complete replica of the Millennium Falcon in 6 hours, a team of 4 Stormtroopers are required. As the competition is in 2 hours' time, how many Stormtroopers would be required in order to complete the replica in time?

8. Pauline and Amitabh are competing against one another in a swimming competition. If Amitabh is twice as fast as Pauline, and Pauline reaches the finish line in 3 minutes, how long did it take Amitabh to reach the finish line?

9. If it takes 9 people 4 minutes to load a truck full of fresh fruit and vegetables, how long would it take 6 people to load the same truck?

10. Rowhurst School is hosting an afternoon fair, where they have promised to have 3 mehndi artists for the 12 children in Year 2. However, it would take the three artists 8 hours in total to decorate all the children's hands. How many more mehndi artists would be needed to decorate the children's hands in only 4 hours?

11. 4 tailors are needed to make a suit in 3 hours. How many tailors would be needed to make the suit in 1 hour?

12. If it takes 6 members of the team to tile a roof in one day, how many days would it take to tile the same roof instead with 4 team members?

13. TFL are planning to paint a large mural on the walls of one of their stations. If three artists take 2 hours to paint a mural on one wall, how many artists would be needed to paint a mural on one wall, in 30 minutes?

14. If 2 pumps are needed to inflate a bouncy castle within 3 hours, in how many hours would the bouncy castle get inflated with only one pump?

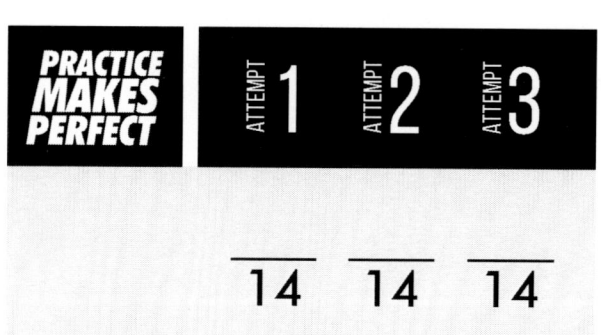

CHAPTER 12
FRACTIONS, DECIMALS & PERCENTAGES

Fill in the gaps below.

Fraction	Decimal	Percentage
½	0.5	50
¼	(1)	(2)
¾	(3)	(4)
(5)	(6)	33.33
(7)	(8)	66.67
⅕	(9)	(10)
⅖	(11)	(12)
⅗	(13)	(14)
(15)	0.8	(16)
⅛	(17)	(18)
⅜	(19)	(20)
⅝	(21)	(22)
(23)	(24)	87.5
1/10	(25)	(26)
3/10	(27)	(28)
7/10	(29)	(30)
(31)	0.9	(32)
1/20	(33)	(34)
7/20	(35)	(36)
13/20	(37)	(38)
13/50	(39)	(40)
39/100	(41)	(42)

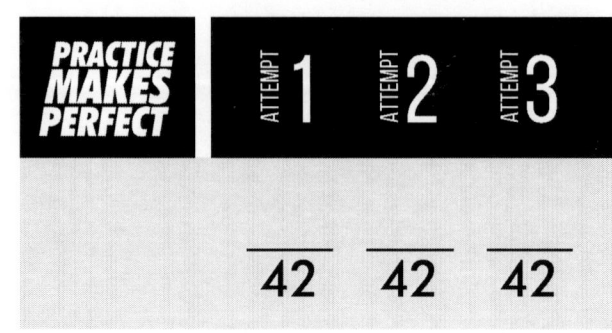

CHAPTER 13
FRACTIONS

Convert the following mixed fractions into improper fractions.

1. $5 \frac{1}{2}$

2. $6 \frac{1}{4}$

3. $2 \frac{1}{2}$

4. $4 \frac{1}{4}$

5. $10 \frac{1}{2}$

6. $3 \frac{1}{6}$

7. $8 \frac{1}{2}$

8. $9 \frac{1}{3}$

9. $11 \frac{1}{2}$

10. $6 \frac{1}{8}$

11. $7 \frac{1}{4}$

12. $8 \frac{1}{7}$

13. $4 \frac{1}{2}$

14. $6 \frac{1}{3}$

15. $6 \frac{1}{4}$

16. $9 \frac{1}{3}$

17. $2 \frac{1}{4}$

18. $1 \frac{1}{4}$

19. $1 \frac{1}{5}$

20. $3 \frac{1}{5}$

21. $4 \frac{1}{8}$

22. $3 \frac{1}{5}$

23. $1 \frac{4}{5}$

24. $1 \frac{1}{6}$

25. $2 \frac{1}{3}$

CHAPTER 13
FRACTIONS
IMPROPER FRACTIONS

Convert the following improper fractions into mixed fractions.

1. 14/5
2. 5/2
3. 21/2
4. 28/3
5. 49/8
6. 54/7
7. 19/3
8. 61/9
9. 22/5
10. 8/3
11. 11/4
12. 16/3
13. 29/4
14. 19/3

15. 28/3
16. 25/2
17. 11/3
18. 9/2
19. 9/4
20. 20/3
21. 17/3
22. 35/2
23. 31/3
24. 29/2
25. 9/5

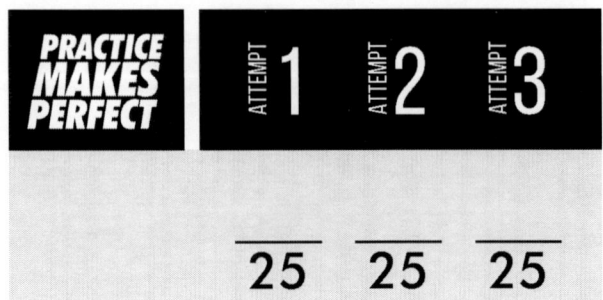

CHAPTER 13
FRACTIONS
ADDITION

Work out the following questions.

1. $\frac{1}{4} + \frac{2}{4}$

2. $\frac{2}{6} + \frac{3}{6}$

3. $\frac{5}{10} + \frac{4}{10}$

4. $\frac{3}{10} + \frac{2}{10}$

5. $\frac{2}{8} + \frac{5}{8}$

6. $\frac{2}{4} + \frac{1}{4}$

7. $\frac{2}{4} + \frac{1}{4}$

8. $\frac{2}{10} + \frac{4}{10}$

9. $\frac{1}{9} + \frac{1}{9}$

10. $\frac{6}{12} + \frac{5}{12}$

11. $\frac{9}{14} + \frac{2}{14}$

12. $\frac{6}{21} + \frac{11}{21}$

13. $\frac{6}{10} + \frac{3}{10}$

14. $\frac{3}{9} + \frac{4}{9}$

15. $\frac{1}{5} + \frac{3}{5}$

16. $\frac{4}{6} + \frac{1}{6}$

17. $\frac{5}{11} + \frac{5}{11}$

18. $\frac{1}{6} + \frac{4}{6}$

19. $\frac{5}{12} + \frac{7}{12}$

20. $\frac{6}{10} + \frac{2}{10}$

21. $\frac{3}{9} + \frac{5}{9}$

22. $\frac{1}{5} + \frac{1}{5}$

23. $\frac{4}{9} + \frac{3}{9}$

24. $\frac{5}{11} + \frac{3}{11}$

25. $\frac{1}{7} + \frac{4}{7}$

CHAPTER 13
FRACTIONS
SUBTRACTION

Work out the following questions.

1. $6/7 - 2/7$

2. $10/10 - 3/10$

3. $10/12 - 3/12$

4. $6/12 - 5/12$

5. $9/14 - 2/14$

6. $3/6 - 1/6$

7. $7/9 - 3/9$

8. $7/10 - 4/10$

9. $10/10 - 5/10$

10. $9/11 - 2/11$

11. $7/12 - 6/12$

12. $9/20 - 2/20$

13. $7/11 - 3/11$

14. $3/6 - 2/6$

15. $5/10 - 2/10$

16. $6/11 - 3/11$

17. $8/12 - 3/12$

18. $11/25 - 7/25$

19. $12/13 - 9/13$

20. $10/11 - 3/11$

21. $5/6 - 2/6$

22. $5/10 - 1/10$

23. $9/11 - 5/11$

24. $8/12 - 5/12$

25. $11/25 - 4/25$

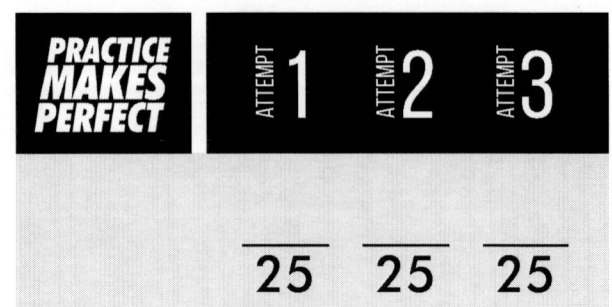

CHAPTER 13
FRACTIONS
ADDITION CONTINUED

Work out the following questions.

1. $\frac{3}{4} + \frac{2}{5}$

2. $\frac{13}{7} + \frac{3}{2}$

3. $\frac{4}{5} + \frac{9}{7}$

4. $\frac{7}{8} + \frac{5}{8}$

5. $\frac{3}{2} + \frac{4}{3}$

6. $\frac{3}{2} + \frac{11}{6}$

7. $\frac{1}{7} + \frac{3}{2}$

8. $\frac{5}{4} + \frac{1}{2}$

9. $\frac{1}{3} + \frac{1}{2}$

10. $\frac{4}{5} + \frac{1}{3}$

11. $\frac{4}{7} + \frac{3}{2}$

12. $\frac{3}{2} + \frac{13}{7}$

13. $\frac{3}{6} + \frac{2}{4}$

14. $\frac{3}{5} + \frac{6}{10}$

15. $\frac{3}{4} + \frac{2}{3}$

16. $\frac{2}{3} + \frac{5}{6}$

17. $\frac{8}{12} + \frac{3}{12}$

18. $\frac{11}{25} + \frac{7}{25}$

19. $\frac{3}{8} + \frac{1}{2}$

20. $\frac{2}{5} + \frac{4}{10}$

21. $\frac{3}{4} + \frac{2}{7}$

22. $\frac{2}{6} + \frac{5}{9}$

23. $\frac{8}{12} + \frac{3}{6}$

24. $\frac{11}{25} + \frac{7}{5}$

25. $\frac{3}{8} + \frac{1}{3}$

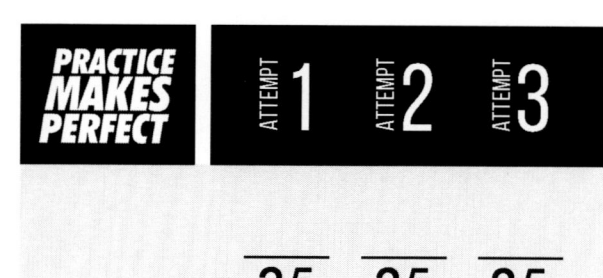

11+ MATHEMATICS

CHAPTER 13
FRACTIONS
SUBTRACTION CONTINUED

Work out the following questions.

1. $\frac{3}{5} - \frac{5}{10}$
2. $\frac{5}{7} - \frac{2}{3}$
3. $\frac{4}{5} - \frac{1}{2}$
4. $\frac{3}{4} - \frac{2}{3}$
5. $\frac{1}{3} - \frac{1}{4}$
6. $\frac{1}{3} - \frac{1}{7}$
7. $\frac{5}{6} - \frac{1}{5}$
8. $\frac{4}{9} - \frac{1}{4}$
9. $\frac{3}{5} - \frac{4}{15}$
10. $\frac{9}{10} - \frac{1}{3}$
11. $\frac{3}{4} - \frac{5}{12}$
12. $\frac{7}{8} - \frac{5}{6}$
13. $\frac{5}{6} - \frac{7}{10}$
14. $\frac{3}{8} - \frac{1}{6}$
15. $\frac{1}{2} - \frac{1}{5}$
16. $\frac{2}{3} - \frac{1}{5}$
17. $\frac{4}{5} - \frac{3}{10}$
18. $\frac{5}{7} - \frac{1}{2}$
19. $\frac{2}{3} - \frac{1}{9}$
20. $\frac{2}{3} - \frac{5}{8}$
21. $\frac{4}{5} - \frac{1}{2}$
22. $\frac{4}{5} - \frac{7}{10}$
23. $\frac{5}{9} - \frac{1}{2}$
24. $\frac{2}{8} - \frac{1}{9}$
25. $\frac{2}{5} - \frac{1}{9}$

PRACTICE MAKES PERFECT

ATTEMPT 1	ATTEMPT 2	ATTEMPT 3
/25	/25	/25

FRACTIONS
MULTIPLICATION

CHAPTER 13

Work out the following questions.

1. 6/7 x 2/7

2. 10/10 x 3/10

3. 10/9 x 3/9

4. 6/12 x 5/12

5. 9/6 x 2/6

6. 3/6 x 1/6

7. 7/9 x 3/9

8. 7/10 x 4/10

9. 10/10 x 5/10

10. 9/11 x 2/8

11. 7/12 x 6/5

12. 9/20 x 2/3

13. 7/11 x 3/9

14. 5/10 x 2/4

15. 6/11 x 3/2

16. 3/4 x 3/4

17. 3/4 x 7/8

18. 3/7 x 9/10

19. 3/5 x 2/4

20. 1/5 x 2/6

21. 3/5 x 3/5

22. 3/7 x 7/8

23. 3/9 x 9/10

24. 3/5 x 2/5

25. 2/7 x 2/5

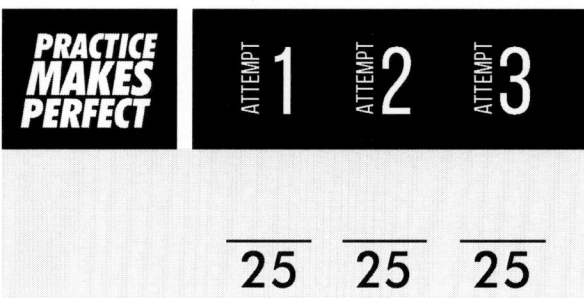

CHAPTER 13
FRACTIONS
DIVISION

Work out the following questions.

1. $\frac{2}{3} \div \frac{2}{4}$

2. $\frac{3}{4} \div \frac{3}{5}$

3. $\frac{17}{3} \div \frac{14}{5}$

4. $\frac{17}{2} \div \frac{14}{3}$

5. $\frac{1}{3} \div \frac{1}{4}$

6. $\frac{23}{3} \div \frac{11}{2}$

7. $\frac{2}{3} \div \frac{2}{5}$

8. $\frac{13}{2} \div \frac{17}{3}$

9. $\frac{2}{4} \div \frac{1}{2}$

10. $\frac{4}{5} \div \frac{1}{2}$

11. $\frac{17}{3} \div \frac{17}{2}$

12. $\frac{35}{4} \div \frac{23}{3}$

13. $\frac{2}{3} \div \frac{1}{2}$

14. $\frac{48}{5} \div \frac{5}{2}$

15. $\frac{3}{5} \div \frac{2}{4}$

16. $\frac{23}{5} \div \frac{38}{4}$

17. $\frac{2}{5} \div \frac{7}{2}$

18. $\frac{38}{5} \div \frac{16}{3}$

19. $\frac{3}{4} \div \frac{1}{3}$

20. $\frac{17}{2} \div \frac{13}{3}$

21. $\frac{11}{5} \div \frac{8}{9}$

22. $\frac{8}{5} \div \frac{7}{3}$

23. $\frac{14}{5} \div \frac{13}{3}$

24. $\frac{13}{4} \div \frac{2}{3}$

25. $\frac{7}{2} \div \frac{14}{3}$

CHAPTER 13
FRACTIONS
MIXED FRACTION ADDITION

Work out the following questions.

1. $1 \frac{1}{2} + 1 \frac{1}{3}$

2. $6 \frac{3}{8} + 9 \frac{1}{24}$

3. $9 \frac{9}{10} + 6 \frac{7}{10}$

4. $4 \frac{6}{7} + 2 \frac{1}{7}$

5. $1 \frac{5}{8} + 3 \frac{3}{8}$

6. $6 \frac{5}{6} + 1 \frac{5}{6}$

7. $1 \frac{3}{8} + 4 \frac{5}{6}$

8. $2 \frac{5}{6} + 4 \frac{1}{3}$

9. $7 \frac{1}{7} + 1 \frac{2}{7}$

10. $3 \frac{1}{4} + 4 \frac{1}{3}$

11. $1 \frac{1}{2} + 1 \frac{2}{5}$

12. $4 \frac{1}{8} + 2 \frac{1}{5}$

13. $3 \frac{1}{4} + 3 \frac{5}{8}$

14. $9 \frac{9}{10} + 2 \frac{3}{5}$

15. $3 \frac{5}{11} + 7 \frac{2}{3}$

16. $5 \frac{2}{8} + 2 \frac{4}{10}$

17. $8 \frac{7}{9} + 5 \frac{9}{11}$

18. $1 \frac{2}{7} + 1 \frac{1}{2}$

19. $5 \frac{1}{2} + 8 \frac{3}{4}$

20. $10 \frac{2}{3} + 7 \frac{1}{7}$

21. $2 \frac{1}{2} + 2 \frac{1}{3}$

22. $3 \frac{3}{8} + 1 \frac{1}{24}$

23. $2 \frac{9}{10} + 3 \frac{7}{10}$

24. $1 \frac{2}{7} + 2 \frac{3}{5}$

25. $1 \frac{5}{6} + 3 \frac{3}{4}$

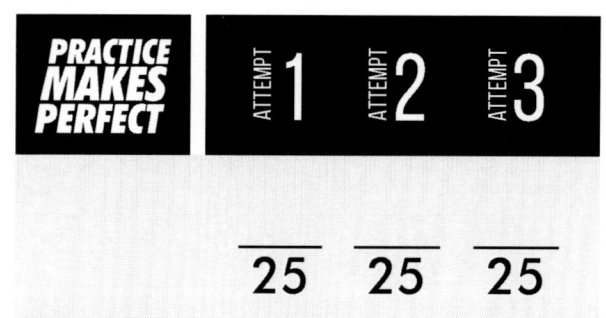

CHAPTER 13
FRACTIONS
MIXED FRACTION SUBTRACTION

Work out the following questions.

1. $4 \frac{3}{4} - 1 \frac{3}{4}$

2. $2 \frac{2}{3} - 1 \frac{1}{3}$

3. $3 \frac{1}{3} - 2 \frac{2}{3}$

4. $4 \frac{2}{7} - 4 \frac{1}{7}$

5. $2 \frac{1}{6} - 1 \frac{3}{4}$

6. $4 \frac{1}{4} - 1 \frac{2}{3}$

7. $3 \frac{5}{6} - 3 \frac{1}{8}$

8. $4 \frac{3}{7} - 1 \frac{2}{3}$

9. $3 \frac{1}{6} - 1 \frac{2}{3}$

10. $8 \frac{7}{8} - 1 \frac{1}{8}$

11. $4 \frac{1}{4} - 1 \frac{3}{4}$

12. $4 \frac{1}{4} - 3 \frac{3}{4}$

13. $4 \frac{2}{5} - 1 \frac{2}{5}$

14. $2 \frac{5}{8} - 1 \frac{5}{6}$

15. $3 \frac{1}{2} - 2 \frac{1}{3}$

16. $4 \frac{2}{5} - 3 \frac{1}{7}$

17. $1 \frac{7}{8} - 1 \frac{5}{6}$

18. $2 \frac{1}{4} - 1 \frac{1}{2}$

19. $3 \frac{1}{2} - 2 \frac{2}{3}$

20. $5 \frac{3}{4} - 5 \frac{1}{4}$

21. $4 \frac{5}{8} - 1 \frac{3}{4}$

22. $1 \frac{1}{2} - 1 \frac{1}{7}$

23. $4 \frac{1}{5} - 2 \frac{1}{7}$

24. $2 - 1 \frac{5}{6}$

25. $2 \frac{1}{5} - 1 \frac{1}{3}$

CHAPTER 13
FRACTIONS
MIXED FRACTION MULTIPLICATION

Work out the following questions.

1. $4\frac{3}{4} \times 1\frac{3}{4}$

2. $2\frac{2}{3} \times 1\frac{1}{3}$

3. $3\frac{1}{3} \times 3\frac{2}{3}$

4. $4\frac{2}{7} \times 2\frac{1}{7}$

5. $2\frac{1}{6} \times 2\frac{3}{4}$

6. $4\frac{1}{4} \times 1\frac{2}{3}$

7. $3\frac{5}{6} \times 1\frac{1}{8}$

8. $4\frac{3}{7} \times 2\frac{2}{3}$

9. $3\frac{1}{6} \times 2\frac{2}{3}$

10. $3\frac{7}{8} \times 2\frac{1}{8}$

11. $4\frac{1}{4} \times 2\frac{3}{4}$

12. $4\frac{1}{4} \times 3\frac{3}{4}$

13. $4\frac{2}{5} \times 2\frac{2}{5}$

14. $2\frac{5}{8} \times 2\frac{5}{6}$

15. $3\frac{1}{2} \times 1\frac{1}{3}$

16. $4\frac{2}{5} \times 2\frac{1}{7}$

17. $1\frac{7}{8} \times 1\frac{5}{6}$

18. $2\frac{1}{4} \times 1\frac{1}{2}$

19. $3\frac{1}{2} \times 2\frac{2}{3}$

20. $5\frac{3}{4} \times 2\frac{1}{4}$

21. $1\frac{2}{5} \times 1\frac{1}{7}$

22. $1\frac{3}{8} \times 1\frac{1}{6}$

23. $3\frac{1}{4} \times 2\frac{1}{2}$

24. $3\frac{1}{3} \times 2\frac{3}{4}$

25. $5\frac{3}{5} \times 2\frac{1}{3}$

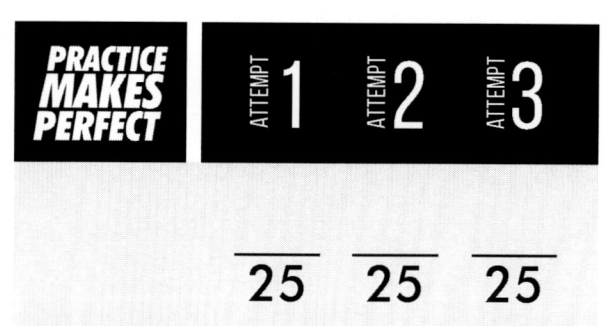

CHAPTER 13
FRACTIONS
MIXED FRACTION DIVISION

Work out the following questions.

1. $2\frac{2}{3} \div 1\frac{2}{4}$
2. $3\frac{3}{4} \div 1\frac{3}{5}$
3. $5\frac{1}{3} \div 2\frac{2}{5}$
4. $2\frac{1}{2} \div 1\frac{1}{3}$
5. $3\frac{1}{3} \div 2\frac{1}{4}$
6. $4\frac{2}{3} \div 3\frac{1}{2}$
7. $3\frac{2}{3} \div 2\frac{2}{5}$
8. $5\frac{1}{2} \div 3\frac{2}{3}$
9. $2\frac{2}{4} \div 1\frac{1}{2}$
10. $3\frac{4}{5} \div 2\frac{1}{2}$
11. $4\frac{2}{3} \div 2\frac{1}{2}$
12. $1\frac{3}{4} \div 1\frac{2}{3}$
13. $4\frac{2}{3} \div 3\frac{1}{2}$
14. $1\frac{4}{5} \div 1\frac{1}{2}$
15. $4\frac{3}{5} \div 3\frac{2}{4}$
16. $1\frac{2}{5} \div 1\frac{3}{4}$
17. $2\frac{2}{5} \div 3\frac{1}{2}$
18. $4\frac{4}{5} \div 3\frac{2}{3}$
19. $6\frac{3}{4} \div 2\frac{1}{3}$
20. $5\frac{5}{6} \div 3\frac{3}{7}$
21. $1\frac{2}{3} \div 1\frac{3}{7}$
22. $2\frac{3}{5} \div 3\frac{1}{3}$
23. $4\frac{4}{20} \div 3\frac{2}{15}$
24. $2\frac{3}{5} \div 2\frac{1}{3}$
25. $1\frac{5}{12} \div 2\frac{3}{6}$

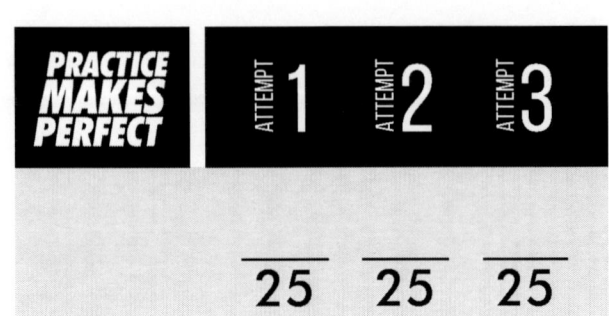

CHAPTER 14

PERCENTAGES

Work out the following questions.

1. What is 10% of 50?
2. What is 10% of 100?
3. What is 10% of 200?
4. What is 20% of 200?
5. What is 20% of 300?
6. What is 20% of 40?
7. What is 30% of 10?
8. What is 30% of 150?
9. What is 30% of 200?
10. What is 15% of 200?
11. What is 15% of 400?
12. What is 25% of 40?
13. What is 25% of 800?
14. What is 25% of 1000?
15. What is 50% of 200?
16. What is 50% of 150?
17. What is 50% of 500?
18. What is 23% of 200?
19. What is 34% of 900?
20. What is 17% of 50?
21. What is 11% of 1000?
22. What is 35% of 200?
23. What is 45% of 500?
24. What is 32% of 300?
25. What is 41% of 800?

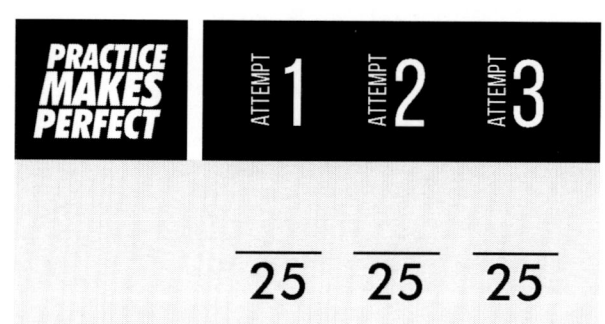

CHAPTER 14
PERCENTAGES
CONTINUED

Work out the following questions.

1. Add 10% to 50
2. Add 10% to 100
3. Add 10% to 80
4. Add 10% to 120
5. Add 20% to 50
6. Add 20% to 70
7. Add 20% to 90
8. Add 20% to 120
9. Add 25% to 200
10. Add 25% to 50
11. Add 25% to 1000
12. Add 25% to 160
13. Add 30% to 150
14. Add 30% to 200
15. Add 30% to 400
16. Add 50% to 250
17. Add 50% to 300
18. Add 50% to 12
19. Add 100% to 100
20. Add 100% to 300
21. Add 150% to 150
22. Add 150% to 300
23. Add 250% to 500
24. Add 120% to 500
25. Add 175% to 1000

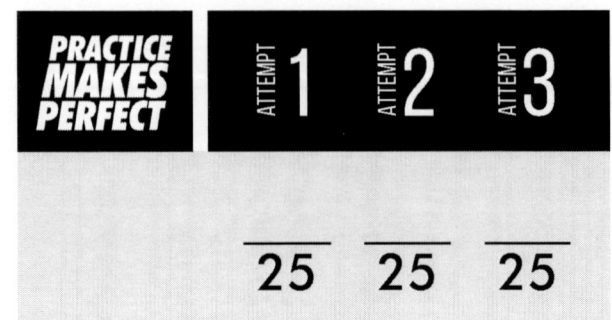

PERCENTAGES
CHAPTER 14
CONTINUED

Work out the following questions.

1. Subtract 10% from 20
2. Subtract 10% from 50
3. Subtract 10% from 80
4. Subtract 15% from 200
5. Subtract 15% from 100
6. Subtract 15% from 150
7. Subtract 20% from 20
8. Subtract 20% from 50
9. Subtract 20% from 500
10. Subtract 30% from 30
11. Subtract 30% from 10
12. Subtract 30% from 120
13. Subtract 30% from 150
14. Subtract 30% from 1500
15. Subtract 40% from 200
16. Subtract 40% from 300
17. Subtract 40% from 80
18. Subtract 50% from 10
19. Subtract 50% from 130
20. Subtract 50% from 190
21. Subtract 80% from 160
22. Subtract 90% from 300
23. Subtract 75% from 100
24. Subtract 10% from 200
25. Subtract 15% from 1000

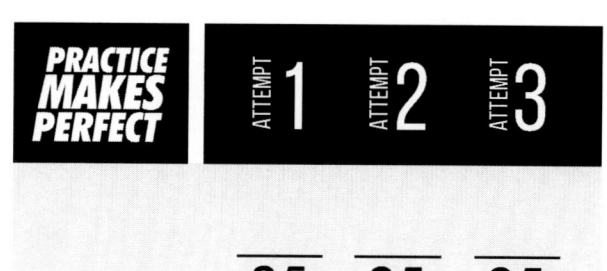

CHAPTER 14
PERCENTAGES
CONTINUED

Work out the following questions.

1. What is 50 out of 200 as a percentage?

2. What is 20 out of 400 as a percentage?

3. What is 40 out of 200 as a percentage?

4. What is 30 out of 200 as a percentage?

5. What is 4 out of 20 as a percentage?

6. What is 80 out of 100 as a percentage?

7. What is 100 out of 500 as a percentage?

8. What is 4 out of 1000 as a percentage?

9. What is 10 out of 100 as a percentage?

10. What is 5 out of 200 as a percentage?

11. What is 40 out of 80 as a percentage?

12. What is 12 out of 60 as a percentage?

13. What is 400 out of 100 as a percentage?

14. What is 20 out of 50 as a percentage?

15. What is 10 out of 2000 as a percentage?

16. What is 25 out of 1000 as a percentage?

17. What is 800 out of 1600 as a percentage?

18. What is 3 out of 1000 as a percentage?

19. What is 15 out of 300 as a percentage?

20. What is 45 out of 45 as a percentage?

21. What is 400 out of 4000 as a percentage?

22. What is 0.5 out of 200 as a percentage?

23. What is 60 out of 1200 as a percentage?

24. What is 0.2 out of 400 as a percentage?

25. What is 1 out of 2000 as a percentage?

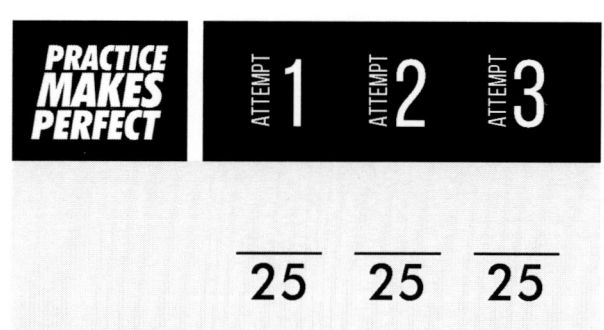

CHAPTER 14
PERCENTAGES
CONTINUED

Work out the following questions.

1. The value of a pen goes up from £10 to £13. What is the percentage change?

2. The value of a pen goes up from £20 to £30. What is the percentage change?

3. The value of a house goes up from £200,000 to £500,000. What is the percentage change?

4. The value of a house goes up from £300,000 to £400,000. What is the percentage change?

5. The value of a house goes up from £250,000 to £500,000. What is the percentage change?

6. The value of a house goes up from £150,000 to £450,000. What is the percentage change?

7. The value of a car depreciates from £20,000 to £16000. What is the percentage change?

8. The value of a car depreciates from £30,000 to £15000. What is the percentage change?

9. The value of a car depreciates from £40,000 to £10,000. What is the percentage change?

10. The value of gold increase from £20/gram to £50/gram. What is the percentage change?

11. The value of gold increase from £30/gram to £33/gram. What is the percentage change?

12. The value of gold increase from £20/gram to £24/gram. What is the percentage change?

13. The value of gold increase from £25/gram to £30/gram. What is the percentage change?

14. During the COVID19 outbreak, the value of a rice bag went up from £40 to £50. What is the percentage change?

15. During the COVID19 outbreak, the value of a pen went up from £20 to £24. What is the percentage change?

16. During the COVID19 outbreak, the value of a shirt went up from £25 to £40. What is the percentage change?

17. The value of Amazon shares jumped from $20 to $30 during the economic crisis in 2020. What is the percentage change?

18. The value of Zoom shares jumped from 90p to £2.70 during the economic crisis in 2020. What is the percentage change?

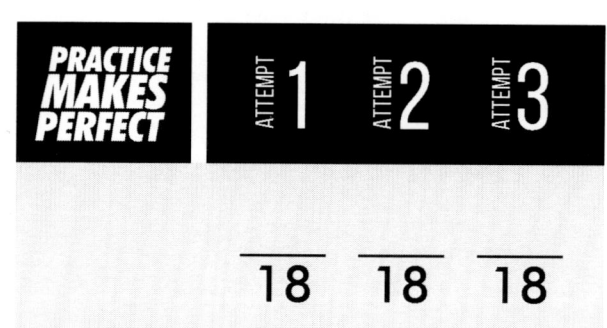

CHAPTER 15
DECIMALS
ADDITION

Work out the following questions.

1. 1.37 + 13.9
2. 0.383 + 15.19
3. 2.6 + 1.11
4. 4.64 + 1.345
5. 3.5 + 222.2
6. 4.004 + 61.3
7. 3.28 + 6.41
8. 7.114 + 25
9. 5.6 + 0.03
10. 3.1 + 121
11. 2.222 + 4.8
12. 13.55 + 6.29
13. 3.221 + 8.9
14. 27.9 + 3.1101
15. 18.43 + 17.99
16. 12.01 + 9.8
17. 19.322 + 8.03
18. 7.18 + 0.003
19. 5.55 + 43.2
20. 0.074 + 1.1114
21. 8.9 + 8.8
22. 23.735 + 1.7
23. 3.39 + 99.9
24. 2.744 + 1.07
25. 3.039 + 909.9

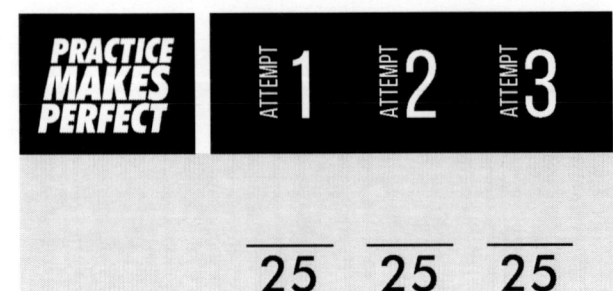

CHAPTER 15
DECIMALS
SUBTRACTION

Work out the following questions.

1. 5.32 – 2.1
2. 67.8 – 18.2
3. 3.9 – 0.22
4. 940.1 – 130.9
5. 8.54 – 3.127
6. 10.6 – 4.115
7. 3.8 – 2.9
8. 11.09 – 5.4
9. 5.46 – 1.39
10. 17.1 – 1.23
11. 2.56 – 0.14
12. 9.79 – 1.1
13. 26.7 – 5.94
14. 3.9 – 3.333
15. 6.23 – 4.3
16. 8.79 – 0.156
17. 13.2 – 4.75
18. 10.4 – 4.8
19. 9.23 – 7.47
20. 2.84 – 1.34
21. 22.9 – 8.8
22. 7.4 – 0.39
23. 28.2 – 13.17
24. 7.04 – 0.039
25. 208.02 – 15.7

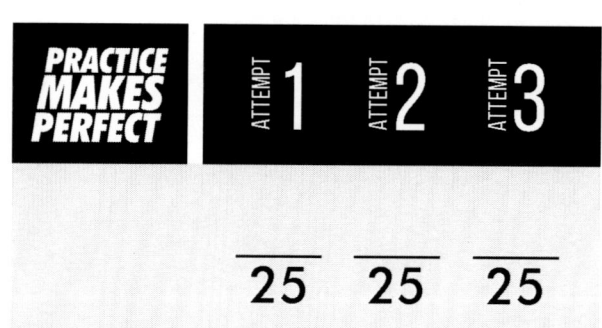

CHAPTER 15
DECIMALS
MULTIPLICATION

Work out the following questions.

1. 11 x 1.2

2. 0.5 x 15

3. 6 x 0.7

4. 1.4 x 2

5. 5 x 0.3

6. 10 x 2.6

7. 0.3 x 4

8. 7 x 0.5

9. 5 x 0.2

10. 3 x 1.5

11. 0.2 x 14

12. 6 x 1.1

13. 0.9 x 4

14. 20 x 0.4

15. 0.8 x 5

16. 4 x 1.2

17. 0.7 x 8

18. 0.07 x 10

19. 5 x 0.6

20. 0.4 x 6

21. 9 x 0.8

22. 0.7 x 12

23. 3 x 0.4

24. 0.7 x 1.2

25. 0.3 x 0.04

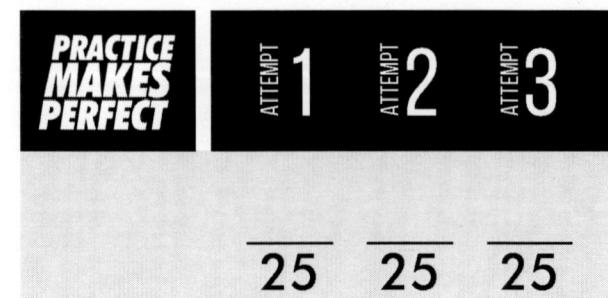

CHAPTER 15
DECIMALS
DIVISION

Work out the following questions.

1. 12 ÷ 0.3
2. 2.4 ÷ 4
3. 20 ÷ 0.04
4. 4.9 ÷ 7
5. 35 ÷ 0.7
6. 0.32 ÷ 10
7. 30 ÷ 0.03
8. 2.2 ÷ 2
9. 56 ÷ 0.7
10. 3.3 ÷ 1.1
11. 1.44 ÷ 12
12. 5.2 ÷ 0.4
13. 0.7 ÷ 2
14. 45 ÷ 0.9
15. 0.81 ÷ 9
16. 24 ÷ 0.06
17. 4.8 ÷ 8
18. 70 ÷ 0.07
19. 55 ÷ 1.1
20. 45 ÷ 1.5
21. 0.36 ÷ 0.3
22. 7.7 ÷ 7
23. 36 ÷ 0.09
24. 0.33 ÷ 0.03
25. 7.77 ÷ 0.7

CHAPTER 16

DECIMAL POINTS

Round each question to the decimal point in the brackets.

1. 1.23 (1dp)

2. 1.364 (2dp)

3. 2.345 (2dp)

4. 2.433 (2dp)

5. 3.1234 (3dp)

6. 4.8765 (3dp)

7. 15.12345 (1dp)

8. 15.2345 (2dp)

9. 14.4564 (3dp)

10. 0.00056 (4dp)

11. 0.234 (1dp)

12. 0.0023 (3dp)

13. 1.89 (1dp)

14. 12.234 (2dp)

15. 134.5674 (3dp)

16. 12.0345 (1dp)

17. 13.3456 (2dp)

18. 14.2324 (3dp)

19. 1.6543 (2dp)

20. 1.0345 (2dp)

21. 1.0098 (3dp)

22. 10.034 (2dp)

23. 9.543 (1dp)

24. 10.057 (2dp)

25. 7.564 (1dp)

PRACTICE MAKES PERFECT | ATTEMPT 1 | ATTEMPT 2 | ATTEMPT 3

$\dfrac{}{25}$ $\dfrac{}{25}$ $\dfrac{}{25}$

CHAPTER 17
SIGNIFICANT FIGURES

Round each question to the significant figure in the brackets.

1. 123 (2sf)
2. 125 (1sf)
3. 3650 (1sf)
4. 4567 (2sf)
5. 57896 (3sf)
6. 65432 (2sf)
7. 765768 (3sf)
8. 2.345 (3sf)
9. 43.225 (3sf)
10. 1.3456 (2sf)
11. 2.3467 (3sf)
12. 0.00023 (1sf)
13. 0.00567 (2sf)
14. 0.0034568 (3sf)
15. 0.00657 (2sf)
16. 1.00345 (3sf)
17. 1.00432 (4sf)
18. 123.1 (2sf)
19. 45003 (2sf)
20. 56008 (3sf)
21. 34321 (1sf)
22. 46505 (2sf)
23. 5675 (3sf)
24. 65550 (2sf)
25. 1234675 (5sf)

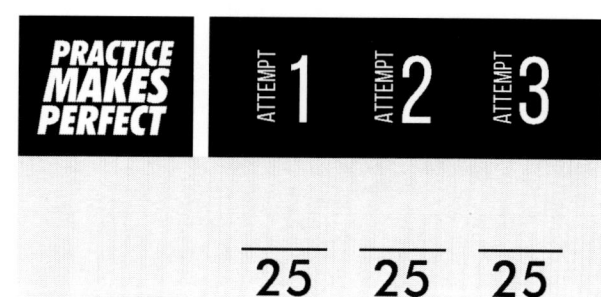

CHAPTER 18
STANDARD FORM

Write the following numbers in standard form.

1. 200
2. 3000
3. 40000
4. 500000
5. 230
6. 2345
7. 34678
8. 543211
9. 32100
10. 4320
11. 50
12. 2000000
13. 0.2
14. 0.03
15. 0.004
16. 0.0005
17. 0.00006
18. 0.12
19. 0.234
20. 0.4567
21. 0.00345
22. 0.02367
23. 0.000568
24. 0.061
25. 0.50063

PRACTICE MAKES PERFECT | ATTEMPT 1 | ATTEMPT 2 | ATTEMPT 3

$\overline{25}$ $\overline{25}$ $\overline{25}$

CHAPTER 19
BIDMAS

Complete the following questions.

1. 2 + 6 x 2
2. 5 + 3 x 4
3. 3 + 9 x 5
4. 4 – 2 x 3
5. 20 – 3 x 6
6. 18 – 4 x 4
7. 12 – 3 x 3
8. 4 x 9 + 5 x 3
9. 5 x 8 + 6 x 2
10. 4 x 10 + 3 x 9
11. 5 x 3 + 4 x 6
12. 4 x 12 – 3 x 5
13. 10 x 10 – 8 x 9
14. 12 x 11 – 13 x 5
15. 8 x 9 + 6 x 3 - 5
16. 3 x 5 + 4 x 9 – 12
17. 6 x 7 – 8 x 3 + 22
18. 20 ÷ 4 + 10 x 2
19. 30 ÷ 6 + 10 ÷ 2
20. 40 ÷ 0.5 + 20 ÷ 2
21. 25 ÷ 5 - 20 ÷ 4
22. 1 x 2 x 3 x 4 x 5 x 6
23. 1 + 2 – 3 + 4 + 5 – 6
24. 4 + 6 x 3 + 5 x 3 – 10
25. 3 + 5 + 8 x 2 + 10 - 20

CHAPTER 19

BIDMAS
CONTINUED

Complete the following questions.

1. $5 + 3 \times (4 + 2) - 9$

2. $4 + 2 \times (3 + 6) - 12$

3. $1^2 + 2^2 + 3^2$

4. $6^2 + 4 \times 3 - 5$

5. $3 \times (9 - 4) + 5^2$

6. $1^2 \times 2^2 + 3^2$

7. $7 \times (2 + 3)^3$

8. $1 \times (3 + 5) \times 7$

9. $1^2 \times (2^2 + 3^2)$

10. $3 + 5 \times (4 + 5)$

11. $3 + 4 \times (4 + 6)^2$

12. $(6 + 5)^2 + (9 - 4)^2$

13. $(2 + 7)^2 + (3 - 1)^2$

14. $12 - 2 + 3^3$

15. $4^2 + 3^3 + 2^4 + 1^5$

16. $9 - 3 \times 5 + 10$

17. $12 \times 11 + 10 \times 5^2$

18. $(4^2 + 3^3) - 2^4 + 1^5$

19. $-2 \times -5 + 10 \times 2$

20. $(4^2 \times 3^2) - 2^3 + 1^5$

21. $-2 \times -4 + 10^2 \times 2^3$

22. $9 + 1 \times (3 + 4) \times 2$

23. $1 \times 12 \times 3 \times 10^3$

24. $-1 \times 5 + 5^2 \times 1^3$

25. $-6 + 1 \times (2 + 4) \times -5$

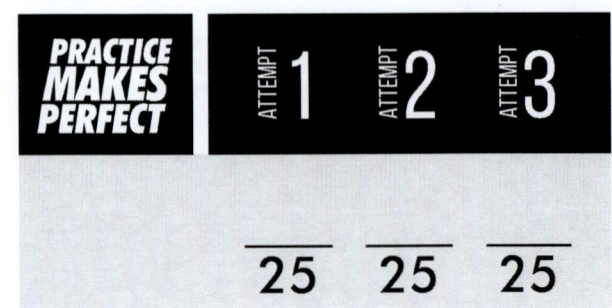

CHAPTER 20
NEGATIVE NUMBERS

Complete the following questions.

1. 5 – 6
2. -4 + 3
3. -6 + 4
4. 9 – 6
5. -6 – 5
6. -5 – 11
7. 10 – 21
8. -6 + 8
9. -6 – 5
10. -10 – 10
11. 40 – 50
12. -16 + 5
13. 26 – 5
14. 14 – 19

15. -2 + 2
16. -3 – 3
17. -8 + 4
18. -4 + 30
19. -6 + 1
20. -8 + 8
21. 12 – 20
22. 13 – 8
23. -6 + 8
24. -12 – 10
25. -13 – 18

11+ MATHEMATICS 55

CHAPTER 20
NEGATIVE NUMBERS
CONTINUED

Complete the following questions.

1. 6 − (-7)
2. 7 + (-3)
3. 9 − (12)
4. 12 − (-3)
5. 20 + (-10)
6. 39 − (+19)
7. 5 − (+3)
8. 20 − (-4)
9. 25 − (-50)
10. 7 + (-70)
11. 17 + (-2)
12. 3 − (+4)
13. 73 − (+32)
14. 49 + (-29)
15. 13 − (-27)
16. 69 − (-42)
17. 76 + (-50)
18. 7 − (-2)
19. 20 + (-3)
20. 41 − (-63)
21. 6 − (-12)
22. 7 − (-11)
23. 20 + (-9)
24. 39 − (-61)
25. 8 − (-12)

CHAPTER 20
NEGATIVE NUMBERS
CONTINUED

Complete the following questions.

1. 5 x (-3)
2. -4 x 6
3. 5 x (-6)
4. -5 x (-5)
5. -7 x 5
6. -8 x (-4)
7. -11 x 2
8. 11 x (-6)
9. -11 x (-11)
10. -12 x (-12)
11. 20 ÷ (-4)
12. -20 ÷ (-5)
13. -10 ÷ (-5)
14. -10 ÷ (-5)

15. 30 ÷ (-6)
16. -40 ÷ (-8)
17. 25 ÷ (-25)
18. -144 ÷ 12
19. -121 ÷ 11
20. -132 ÷ (-12)
21. -12 ÷ (-12)
22. -121 ÷ 11
23. -121 ÷ (-11)
24. -132 ÷ (-2)
25. -6 ÷ (-12)

CHAPTER 21

ALGEBRA

Simplify the following questions.

1. $2t + 3 + 4t + 5$

2. $2a + 3b + 4ab + 5a + 6a$

3. $3t - 5 + 4t - 6$

4. $3s + 2t + 5s + 4t$

5. $7a + 3b + a + 2b$

6. $5m + n + 4m + 2n$

7. $z + 3y + 6z - 2y$

8. $6a + 2b + 5a - 7b$

9. $3a - 2b + a - 3b$

10. $3ab + 2a + 4ab - 2b$

11. $5ab - 2b + ab - 3b$

12. $6y + 2fy - 4y - 7f$

13. $5v + 4 + 2v + 1$

14. $3q + 8q - 2q^2$

15. $3l - l + 5l - 7l$

16. $8u - 10u + 7u + 5u$

17. $3c - c + 5c - 7c$

18. $ab + ab + ab$

19. $12pq - 5p + 2pq + 3q$

20. $8jh + jh - 3jh$

21. $6p + 2t - 4p - 6t$

22. $2ab + 3ab - 5ab$

23. $1pq - 6p + 9pq + 5q$

24. $4jh + jh - 8jh$

25. $-2p + 8t - 4p - 6t$

CHAPTER 21
ALGEBRA
CONTINUED

Open the brackets for the following questions.

1. 7(x + 2)
2. 9(x - 3)
3. 14(x + 2)
4. -3(x - 3)
5. -9(x + 6)
6. 10(x + 4)
7. -25(x + 4)
8. 7(x + 1)
9. -3(x - 2)
10. 7(x + 11)
11. -2(x + 16)
12. 3(x + 42)
13. -2(x + 4)
14. -4(x - 3)
15. -9(x + 25)
16. 7(x + 20)
17. 7(x + 6)
18. -3(x + 3)
19. -2(x + 7)
20. -4(x + 5)
21. -5(x + 9)
22. -3(x - 5)
23. -2(x - 10)
24. -3(x - 5)
25. -5(x + 6)

CHAPTER 21
ALGEBRA
CONTINUED

Work out the value of 'a' in the following questions.

1. $5a = 75$
2. $6a = 66$
3. $8a = 64$
4. $4a = 20$
5. $9a = 81$
6. $9a = 27$
7. $10a = 100$
8. $11a = 121$
9. $3a = 12$
10. $5a = 20$
11. $4a = 36$
12. $20a = 100$
13. $25a = 125$
14. $11a = 88$

15. $60a = 120$
16. $7a = 84$
17. $12a = -144$
18. $9a = -81$
19. $11a = -55$
20. $-12a = 108$
21. $15a = -30$
22. $8a = -64$
23. $11a = -77$
24. $-12a = -96$
25. $-a = 30$

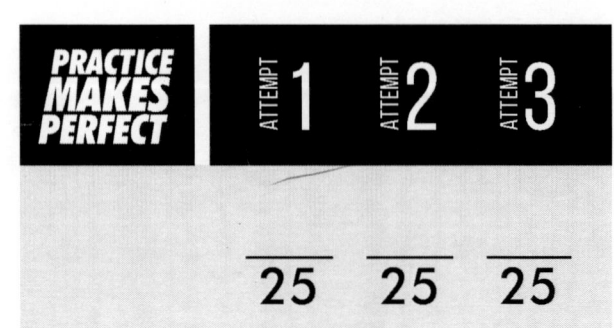

CHAPTER 21
ALGEBRA
CONTINUED

Work out the value of 'a' in the following questions.

1. a ÷ 5 = 50
2. a ÷ 5 = 10
3. a ÷ 5 = 20
4. a ÷ 8 = 50
5. 2a ÷ 5 = 40
6. a ÷ 2 = 8
7. a ÷ 7 = 8
8. 3a ÷ 5 = 30
9. 5a ÷ 3 = 25
10. 3a ÷ 5 = 12
11. 4a ÷ 3 = 16
12. a ÷ 5 = 9
13. a ÷ 5 = 100
14. a ÷ 4 = 60
15. 2a ÷ 5 = 8
16. 6a ÷ 5 = 18
17. a ÷ 10 = 50
18. a ÷ 100 = 100
19. a ÷ 4 = 7
20. a ÷ 2 = 200
21. a ÷ 7 = 60
22. 2a ÷ 3 = 12
23. 6a ÷ 10 = 6
24. a ÷ 8 = 500
25. a ÷ 1000 = 1000

CHAPTER 21
ALGEBRA
CONTINUED

Work out the value of 'T' in the following questions.

1. T + 6 = 10

2. T + 4 = 12

3. T + 12 = 20

4. T + 7 = 42

5. T + 25 = 35

6. T + 32 = 50

7. T + 18 = 23

8. T + 39 = 42

9. T + 13 = 17

10. T + 26 = 40

11. T + 3 = 12

12. T + 7 = 37

13. T + 6 = 19

14. T + 13 = 13

15. T + 41 = 27

16. T + 3 = 34

17. T + 17 = 14

18. T + 39 = 7

19. T + 3 = 2

20. T + 23 = 33

21. T - 2 = -34

22. T - 16 = -14

23. T - 39 = -9

24. T - 3 = -5

25. T - 25 = 43

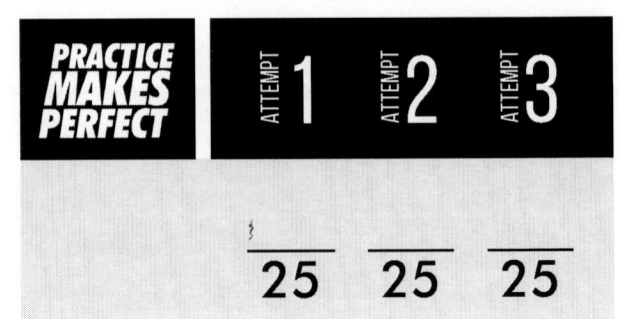

CHAPTER 21

ALGEBRA
CONTINUED

Work out the value of 'T' in the following questions.

1. T - 3 = 12
2. T - 5 = 10
3. T - 4 = 12
4. T - 32 = 50
5. T - 13 = 2
6. T - 25 = 10
7. T - 17 = 14
8. T - 5 = 5
9. T - 20 = 15
10. T - 5 = 11
11. T - 22 = 10
12. T - 11 = 5
13. T - 9 = 6
14. T - 6 = 8
15. T - 20 = 10
16. T - 19 = 18
17. T - 21 = 14
18. T - 11 = 23
19. T - 29 = 33
20. T - 21 = 60
21. T - 18 = 18
22. T - 25 = 4
23. T - 9 = 25
24. T - 23 = 35
25. T - 41 = 70

CHAPTER 21
ALGEBRA
CONTINUED

Work out the value of 't' in the following questions.

1. $2t + 6 = 10$
2. $2t + 8 = 22$
3. $3t + 9 = 27$
4. $2t + 11 = 19$
5. $4t + 2 = 18$
6. $5t + 101 = 21$
7. $2t + 9 = 49$
8. $5t + 44 = 54$
9. $4t + 19 = 21$
10. $2t + 18 = 24$
11. $10t + 12 = 22$
12. $2t + 11 = 29$
13. $2t + 1 = 5$
14. $4t + 6 = 12$
15. $8t + 8 = 16$
16. $16t + 20 = 24$
17. $5t + 199 = 209$
18. $4t + 44 = 52$
19. $3t + 8 = 14$
20. $2t + 10 = 18$
21. $3t + 30 = 90$
22. $5t + 40 = 55$
23. $3t + 8 = 9$
24. $2t + 20 = 18$
25. $4t + 40 = 60$

CHAPTER 21

ALGEBRA
CONTINUED

Work out the value of 't' in the following questions.

1. 3t + 5 = -10
2. 2t + 10 = -18
3. 5t + 7 = -23
4. 3t + 8 = -10
5. 8t + 11 = -29
6. 7t + 3 = -25
7. 3t + 3 = -9
8. 3t + 12 = -21
9. 3t + 4 = -17
10. 3t + 6 = -36
11. 5t + 2 = -33
12. -4t + 14 = 26
13. -5t + 100 = 130
14. -3t + 200 = 260
15. -3t + 9 = 24
16. -5t + 20 = 140
17. -6t + 40 = 190
18. -2t + 52 = 58
19. -3t + 19 = 22
20. -3t + 44 = 50
21. -4t + 20 = 60
22. -10t + 48 = 58
23. -3t + 18 = 27
24. -5t + 44 = 64
25. -2t + 20 = 80

CHAPTER 21

ALGEBRA
CONTINUED

Work out the value of 't' in the following questions.

1. 2t - 5 = 3
2. 3t - 10 = 2
3. 5t - 8 = 2
4. 4t - 50 = 50
5. 7t - 4 = 10
6. 8t - 7 = 9
7. 2t - 3 = 37
8. 4t - 1 = 99
9. 11t - 11 = 11
10. 9t - 80 = 370
11. 4t - 9 = 11
12. 2t - 15 = 25
13. 3t - 30 = 0
14. 2t - 20 = 2
15. 3t - 13 = 17
16. 2t - 17 = -2
17. 4t - 19 = -3
18. 2t - 40 = -60
19. 5t - 100 = -300
20. 2t - 200 = 600
21. 7t - 20 = 120
22. 3t - 40 = -10
23. 2t - 10 = -200
24. 3t - 300 = 600
25. 5t - 30 = 120

CHAPTER 21
ALGEBRA
CONTINUED

Work out the value of 't' in the following questions.

1. 3t - 5 = -20
2. 2t - 10 = -100
3. 3t - 15 = -45
4. 5t - 20 = -50
5. 4t - 2 = -11
6. 3t - 4 = -34
7. 6t - 6 = -24
8. 2t - 8 = -14
9. 3t - 3 = -6
10. 2t - 4 = -10
11. 5t - 9 = -4
12. -2t - 8 = 108
13. -3t - 4 = 8
14. -4t - 8 = 92
15. -3t - 12 = -102
16. -5t - 16 = 74
17. -3t - 6 = 120
18. -2t - 12 = 24
19. -4t - 18 = 12
20. -3t - 8 = 31
21. -4t - 100 = 100
22. -6t - 200 = 400
23. -5t - 80 = 320
24. -5t - 12 = 38
25. -2t - 16 = 22

CHAPTER 21

ALGEBRA
CONTINUED

Work out the value of 't' in the following questions.

1. 3t - 5 = t - 20

2. 2t - 10 = t - 100

3. 3t - 15 = t - 45

4. 5t - 20 = t - 50

5. 4t - 2 = t - 11

6. 3t - 4 = t - 32

7. 6t + 6 = t - 14

8. 2t - 8 = -14 + t

9. 3t - 3 = -6 + t

10. 2t - 4 = -10 + t

11. 5t - 9 = -4 + 4t

12. -2t - 8 = 106 + t

13. -3t - 4 = 8 - t

14. -4t - 8 = 91 - t

15. -3t - 12 = -102 - 2t

16. -5t - 16 = 74 + t

17. -3t - 6 = 120 - t

18. -2t - 12 = 24 + 2t

19. -4t - 18 = 12 - 2t

20. -3t - 8 = 31 - 2t

21. 2t + 8 = t - 6

22. 3t - 4 = t + 8

23. 4t - 3 = t + 6

24. 2t - 10 = t + 7

25. 3t - 3 = t + 7

CHAPTER 21
ALGEBRA
SIMULTANEOUS EQUATIONS

Work out the value of 'a' and the value of 'b'.

1. $2a + b = 4$
    $a + 2b = 5$

2. $2a + b = 5$
    $a + 2b = 3$

3. $2a + b = 7$
    $a + 2b = 8$

4. $3a + b = 10$
    $a + 4b = 7$

5. $3a + 2b = 16$
    $2a + 2b = 12$

6. $2a + 3b = 16$
    $a + 2b = 9$

7. $2a + b = 20$
    $a + 5b = 28$

8. $2a + b = 25$
    $a + 6b = 40$

9. $2a - 2b = 8$
    $4a + 2b = 4$

10. $4a + b = 21$
    $a + 2b = 0$

11. $2a + 2b = 14$
    $3a + 3b = 21$

12. $4a + 2b = 32$
    $5a + 3b = 43$

13. $3a + 2b = 44$
    $a + 4b = 48$

14. $2a + 5b = 36$
    $5a + 2b = 27$

15. $3a + 4b = 55$
    $4a + 3b = 50$

16. $5a + 2b = 90$
    $10a + 3b = 160$

17. $2a + 10b = 220$
    $1a + 2b = 50$

18. $2a + 3b = 4$
    $3a + 6b = 9$

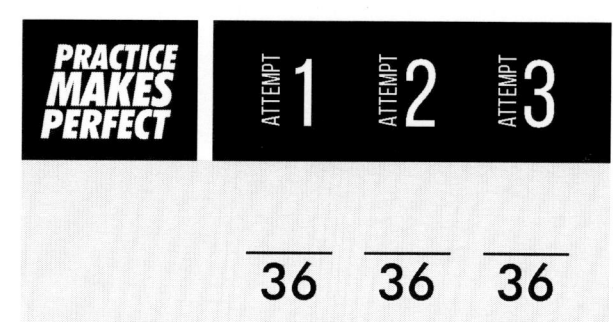

CHAPTER 21
ALGEBRA
CONTINUED

Complete the following questions using algebra.

1. The perimeter of a rectangle is 30cm. If the length is double the width, calculate the length, width and area of the rectangle.

2. The area of a triangle is 21cm², and the base of the triangle is 6cm. Calculate the height of the triangle.

3. The area of a rectangle is 27cm². If the length is three times the width, calculate the length, width and perimeter of the rectangle.

4. The length of a rectangle is x cm, and the width is four times the length. If the area of the rectangle is 16cm², calculate the length, width and perimeter of the rectangle.

5. The height of a triangle is twice the base of the triangle, and the area of the triangle is 25cm². Using this information, calculate the height and the base of the triangle.

6. The perimeter of a regular, symmetrical kite is 56cm. The kite has two short sides equal in value and two long sides also equal in value. One long side of the kite is three times the length of one short side of the kite. Using this information, calculate the value of the long and short sides of the kite.

7. The area of a regular parallelogram is 200cm². If the parallelogram has a height that is twice the base, calculate the values of the base and height of the parallelogram.

8. The area of a triangle is 48cm², and the base of the triangle is 8cm. Using this information, calculate the height of the triangle.

9. The perimeter of a regular, symmetrical kite is 44cm. The kite has two short sides equal in value and two long sides also equal in value. One long side of the kite is ten times the length of one short side of the kite. Using this information, calculate the value of the long and short sides of the kite.

10. The perimeter of a rectangle is 18cm. If the length is half the value of the width, calculate the length, width and area of the rectangle.

11. The area of a regular parallelogram is 72cm². If the parallelogram has a height that is twice the base, calculate the values of the base and height of the parallelogram.

12. The area of a triangle is 32cm², and the base of the triangle is one quarter of the value of the height. Using this information, calculate the base and the height of the triangle.

13. The area of a rectangle is 48cm². If the length is a third of the value of the width, calculate the length, width and perimeter of the rectangle.

14. The length of a rectangle is y cm, and the width is eleven times the length. If the area of the rectangle is 99cm², calculate the length, width and perimeter of the rectangle.

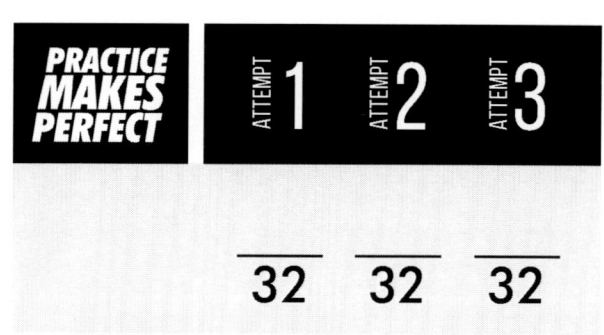

CHAPTER 22
AREA & PERIMETER

Find the area and perimeter of the following shapes.

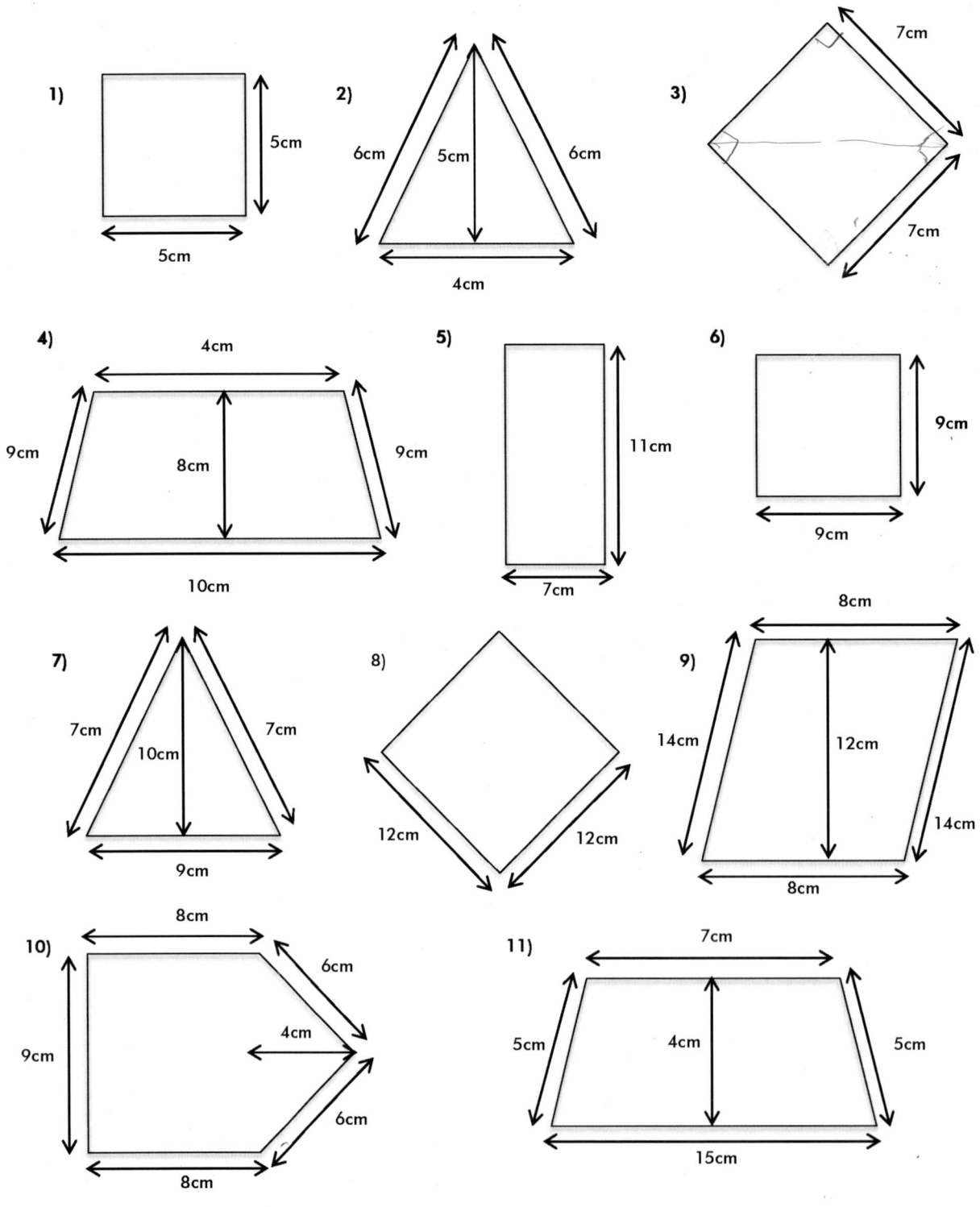

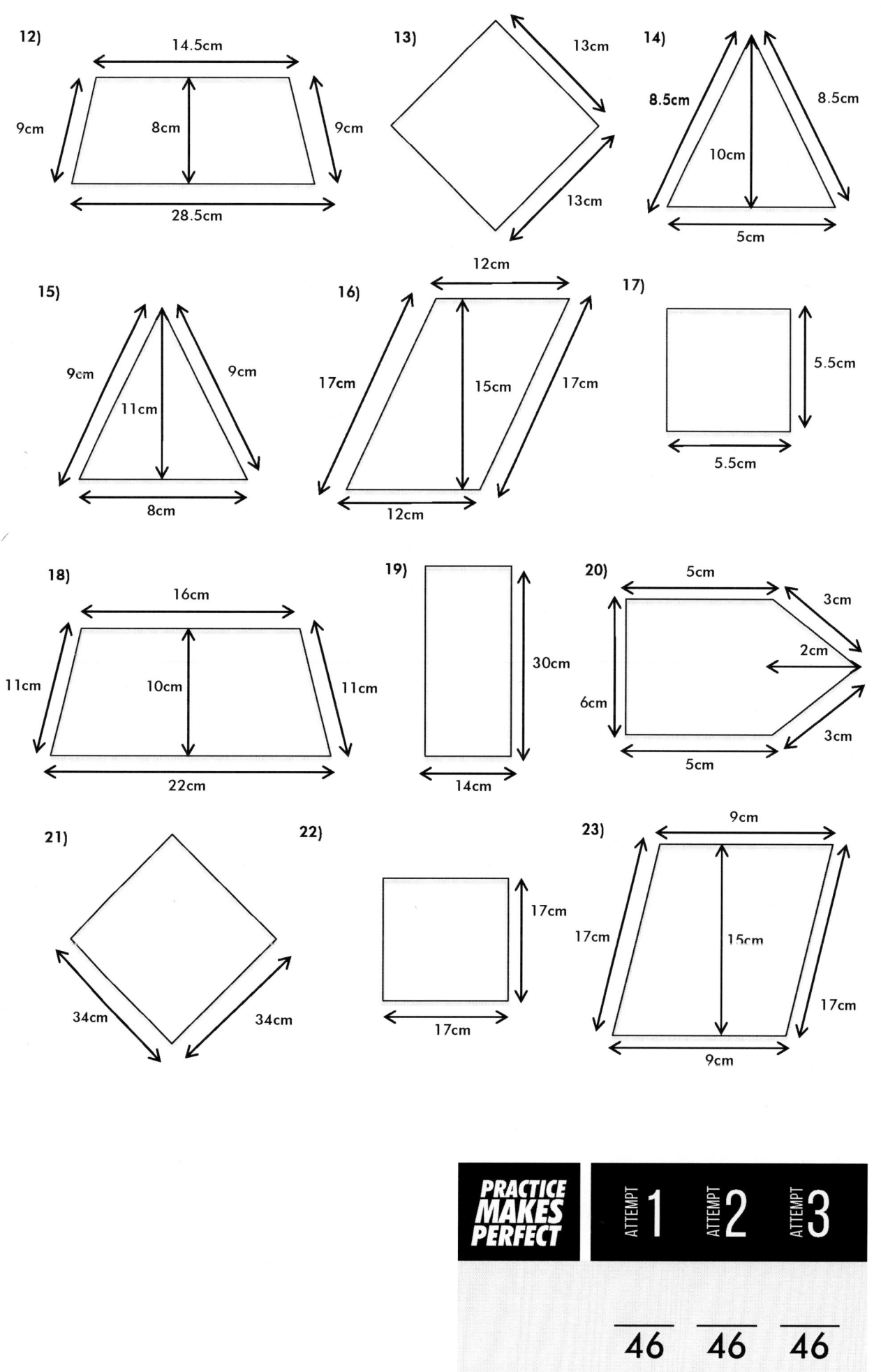

CHAPTER 23
AREA OF COMPOUND SHAPES

Find the area of the following shapes.

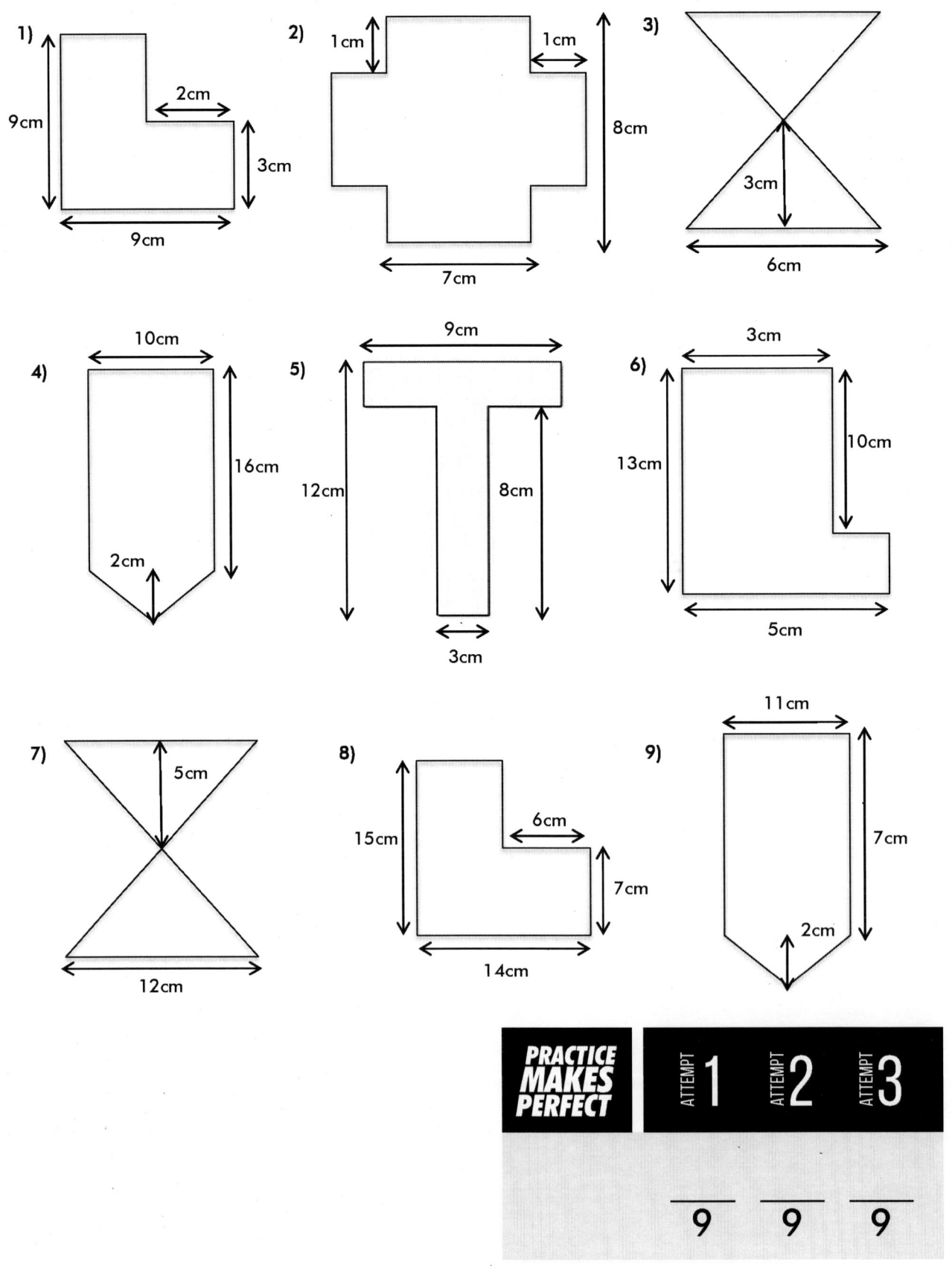

CHAPTER 24
CIRCLES

Work out the following questions, assuming pi is 3.

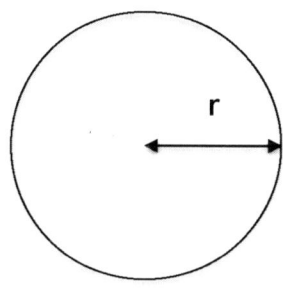

1. What is the area and circumference of the circle if r = 12cm?
2. What is the area and circumference of the circle if r = 3m?
3. What is the area and circumference of the circle if r = 9mm?
4. What is the area and circumference of the circle if r = 20mm?
5. What is the area and circumference of the circle if r = 7cm?

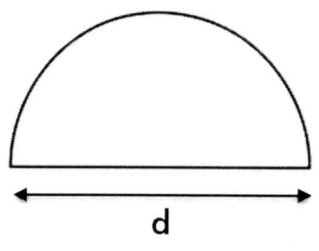

6. What is the area and circumference of the semi-circle if d = 20mm?
7. What is the area and circumference of the semi-circle if d = 8m?
8. What is the area and circumference of the semi-circle if d = 12cm?
9. What is the area and circumference of the semi-circle if d = 44cm?
10. What is the area and circumference of the semi-circle if d = 32mm?

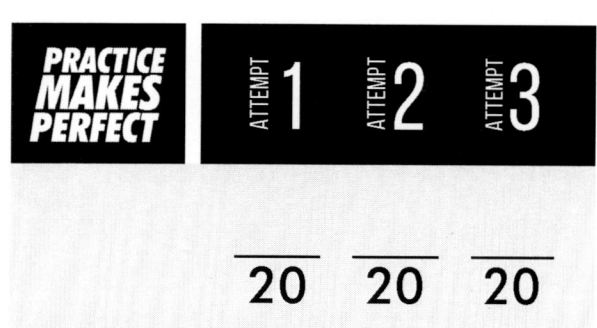

CHAPTER 25
CUBOIDS

Use the diagram to calculate the surface area and volume of the cuboid with the given units in each question.

1. a = 5cm, b = 11cm and c = 3cm

2. a = 10mm, b = 22mm and c = 4mm

3. a = 8mm, b = 15mm and c = 3mm

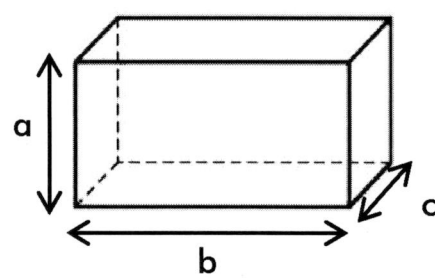

4. a = 20cm, b = 30cm and c = 10cm

5. a = 7cm, b = 16cm and c = 5cm

6. a = 15cm, b = 25cm and c = 2cm

7. a = 50mm, b = 25mm and c = 10mm

8. a = 13cm, b = 15cm and c = 6cm

9. a = 8cm, b = 14cm and c = 2cm

10. a = 5mm, b = 18mm and c = 1mm

11. a = 45mm, b = 60mm and c = 20mm

12. a = 12cm, b = 35cm and c = 7cm

13. a = 100cm, b = 120cm and c = 50cm

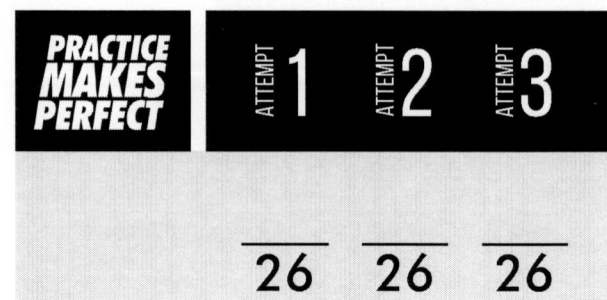

CHAPTER 26
CYLINDERS

Find the volume of the following cylinders, assuming that pi = 3.

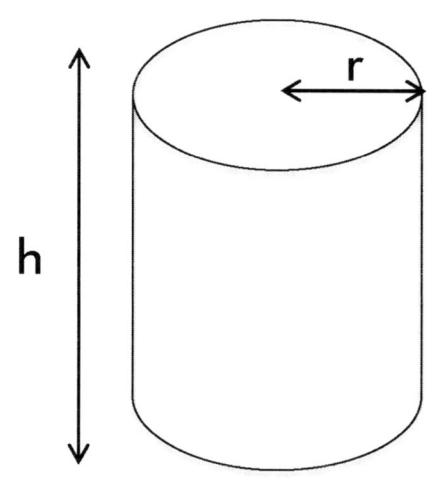

1. h = 12cm and r = 3cm
2. h = 10cm and r = 2cm
3. h = 14cm and r = 5cm
4. h = 9cm and r = 4cm
5. h = 20cm and r = 1cm
6. h = 15cm and r = 2cm
7. h = 5cm and r = 5cm
8. h = 22cm and r = 3cm
9. h = 18cm and r = 6cm
10. h = 30cm and r = 10cm
11. h = 11cm and r = 4cm
12. h = 17cm and r = 2cm
13. h = 23cm and r = 1cm

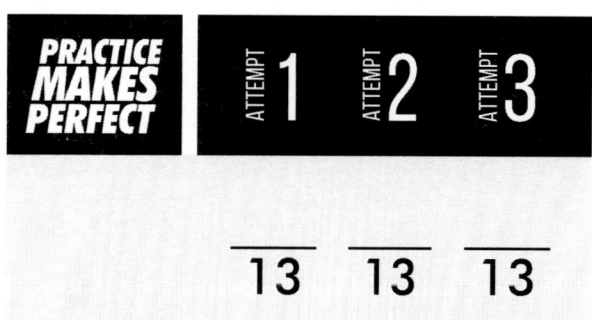

CHAPTER 27
ANGLES

Find the value of the unknown angle.

1)

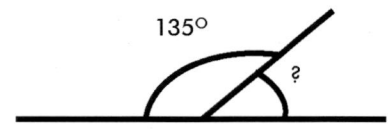

2)

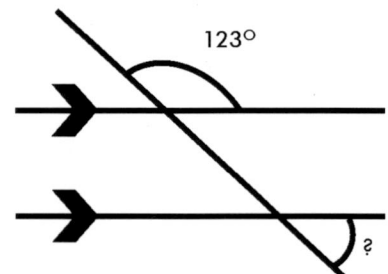

3)

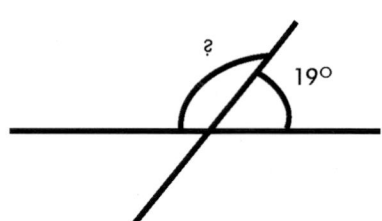

4)

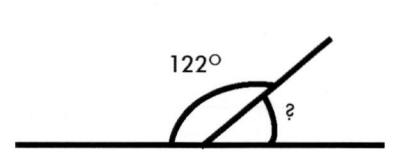

5)

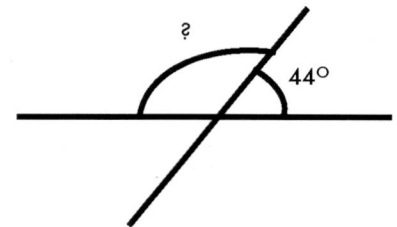

6)

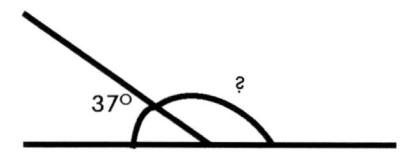

7)

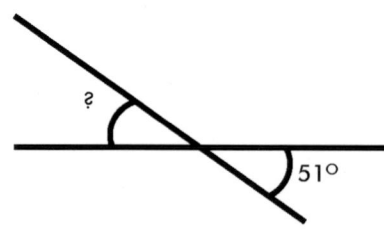

8)

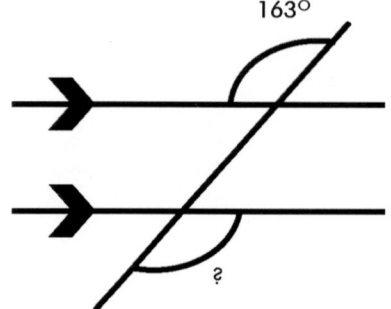

9)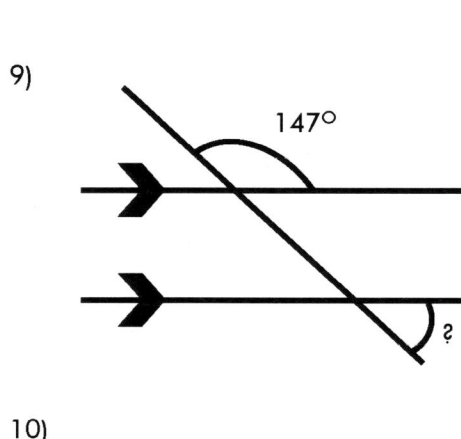

13)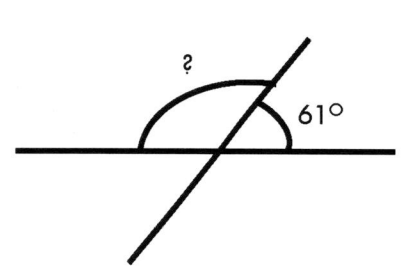

10) 108° ?

14)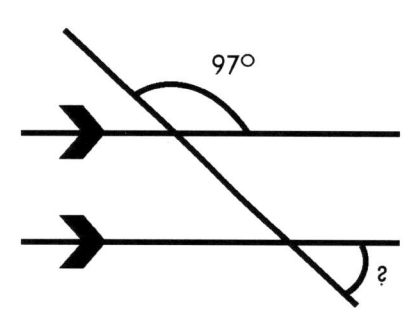

11) 35° ?

15)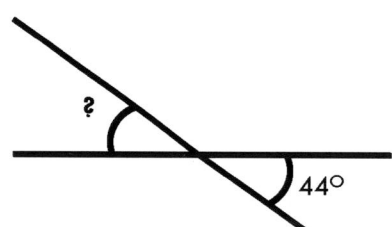

12)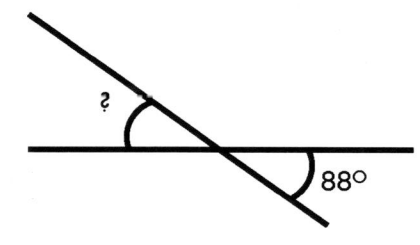

16)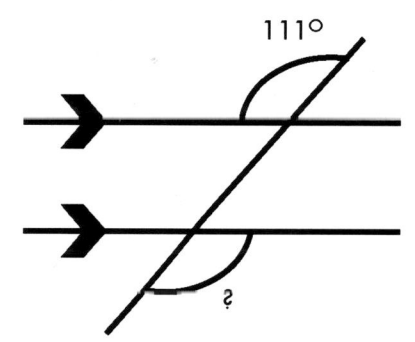

PRACTICE MAKES PERFECT	ATTEMPT 1	ATTEMPT 2	ATTEMPT 3
	/16	/16	/16

CHAPTER 27
ANGLES

Calculate the value of each interior angle and exterior angle in the following REGULAR shapes. The shapes are not drawn to scale.

1)

2)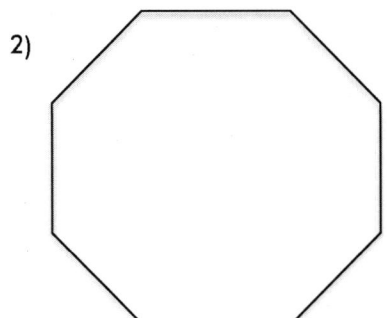

3)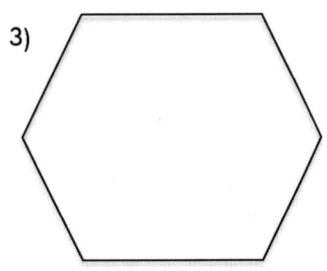

4)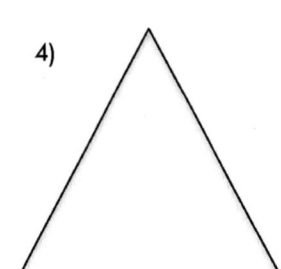

5)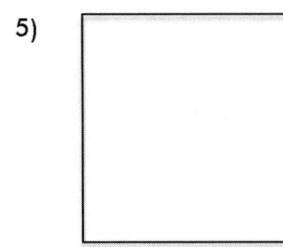

6)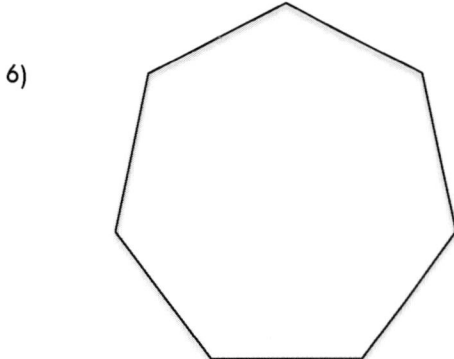

7)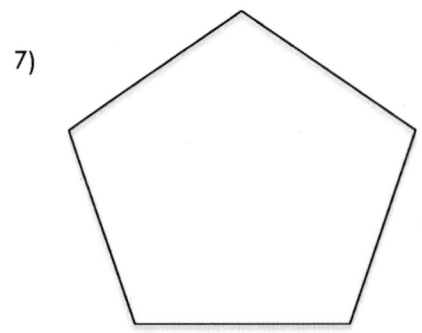

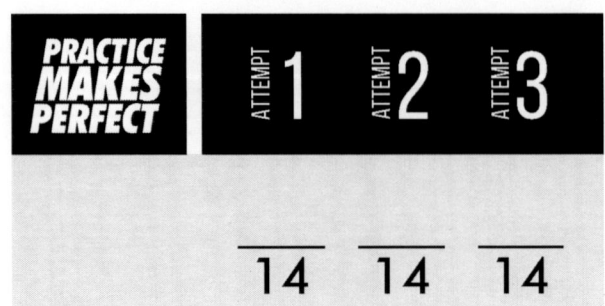

CHAPTER 28
3D SHAPES

For each of the following shapes, state the number of faces (A), the number of vertices (B) and the number of edges (C).

1. Cube

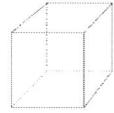

2. Cuboid

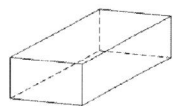

3. Cylinder

4. Sphere

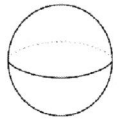

5. Cone

6. Hemisphere

7. Square-Based Pyramid

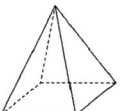

8. Tetrahedron

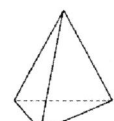

9. Octahedron

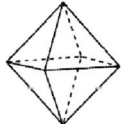

10. Triangular Prism

11. Hexagonal Prism

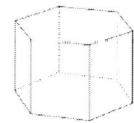

12. Octagonal Prism

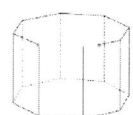

Three dimensional shapes can be classified by the number of faces, vertices and edges. Faces are surfaces in shape and can be either flat or rounded.

Edges are the sides of the shape where two faces meet.

Vertices are the corners or points of the shape.

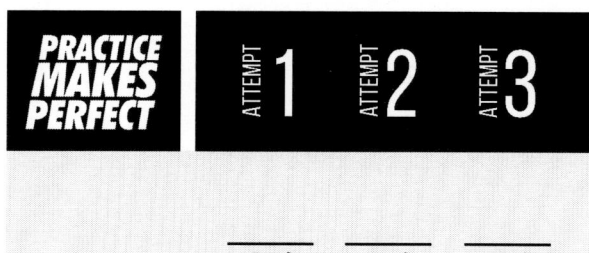

11+ MATHEMATICS 81

CHAPTER 29
PROBABILITY

There is a bag filled with a number of marbles in different colours. There are 20 marbles in total. Of these, 7 of the marbles are blue, 5 of the marbles are red, 2 of the marbles are green, and the remaining are yellow.

1. What is the probability of picking a red marble from the bag?

2. What is the probability of picking a yellow marble from the bag?

3. What is the probability of picking a blue marble from the bag?

4. What is the probability of picking a green marble from the bag?

5. Calculate the probability of picking either a yellow, red or green marble from the bag.

6. What is the probability of not picking a yellow marble from the bag?

7. What is the probability of not picking a yellow or green marble from the bag?

8. What is the probability of not picking a red or blue or green marble from the bag?

9. What is the probability of picking a green marble from the bag, and putting the marble back, before picking a yellow marble from the bag?

10. What is the probability of picking either a green or blue marble from the bag, putting the marble back, and then picking a red marble from the bag?

11. Calculate the probability of picking a yellow marble from the bag, returning the marble to the bag and consequently picking either a blue or yellow marble from the bag.

12. What is the probability of picking a red marble from the bag, and putting the marble on the side, before picking a green marble from the bag?

13. What is the probability of picking a green or blue marble from the bag, putting the marble on the side, and consequently picking a yellow marble from the bag?

14. Calculate the probability of picking a blue marble from the bag, putting the marble on the side, and then picking either a green or yellow marble from the bag.

15. Calculate the probability of picking two red marbles from the bag in a row, replacing the marble after each pick.

16. Calculate the probability of picking two green marbles from the bag in a row, without replacing the marble after each pick.

17. What is the probability of picking a pink marble from the bag?

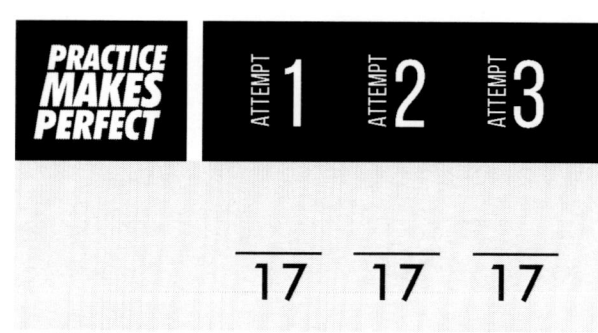

CHAPTER 29
PROBABILITY
CONTINUED

The following questions are in reference to a standard 6-faced die. Each of the faces are labelled from 1-6, and the probability of landing on any face is equal and constant. Each roll is independent of another.

1. What is the probability of rolling the die and landing on an even number?

2. What is the probability of rolling the die and landing on an odd number?

3. What is the probability of rolling the die and landing on a prime number?

4. What is the probability of rolling the die and landing on a 3?

5. What is the probability of rolling the die and landing a number greater than 4?

6. What is the probability of rolling either an odd number or a four on a die?

7. Calculate the probability of rolling the die and landing on a multiple of three, and then rolling the die again and landing on a multiple of two.

8. What is the probability of rolling the die and landing on a three, and then rolling the die again and landing on a five?

9. What is the probability of rolling the die three times and landing on a five, two and six consecutively?

10. What is the probability of rolling the die and landing on a one, three or six and rolling the die again and landing on a one, four or five?

11. Calculate the probability of rolling the die and landing on an even or an odd number, and then rolling the die again and landing on an odd or an even number.

12. What is the probability of rolling the die three times, and rolling either a three or a four on the three rolls consecutively?

13. Calculate the probability of rolling the die and landing on a number greater than 6.

14. What is the probability of rolling a die and landing on a 10?

For the following questions, two dice are rolled and the numbers on the dice are added together. Eg die 1 = 5; die 2 = 3. Therefore, the total is 8.

15. What is the probability of rolling a total of 10 on 2 dice?

16. What is the probability of rolling a total of greater than 9 on 2 dice?

17. What is the probability of rolling a total of 4 or less on 2 dice?

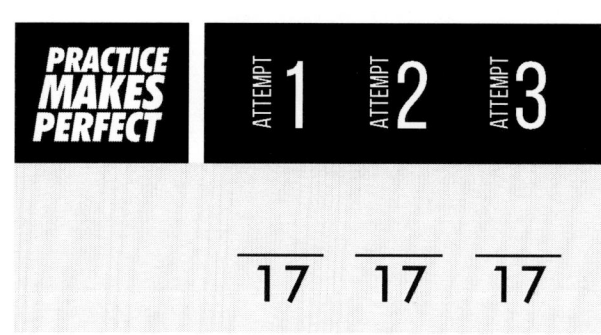

CHAPTER 29

PROBABILITY
CONTINUED

A standard deck of cards consists of 52 cards. These cards are separated into four different 'suits': Clubs (black), Spades (black), Hearts (red) and Diamonds (red).

Each suit consists of 13 cards: 2, 3, 4, 5, 6, 7, 8, 9, 10, Jack, Queen, King, Ace.

1. What is the probability of picking a red card from the deck?

2. What is the probability of picking a black card from the deck?

3. What is the probability of picking a diamond card from the deck?

4. What is the probability of picking a heart card from the deck?

5. What is the probability of picking an odd numbered card from the deck?

6. What is the probability of picking an even numbered card from the deck?

7. What is the probability of picking a prime numbered card from the deck?

8. What is the probability of picking either an Ace or a King from the deck?

9. What is the probability of picking a Queen from the deck?

10. What is the probability of picking a King from the deck?

11. What is the probability of picking a numbered card from the deck?

12. Calculate the probability of picking a Queen, returning it back to the standard deck, and then picking an Ace from the standard deck.

13. Calculate the probability of picking a black card, and returning it back to the standard deck, before then picking out a Jack from the standard deck.

14. Calculate the probability of picking a red King, retuning it back to the deck, and then picking a 2 from the standard deck.

15. What is the probability of picking a 10 from a standard deck and placing the card aside, before picking a 3 from the deck?

16. Calculate the probability of picking a black card from a standard deck, placing the card aside, and then picking an Ace of Diamonds from the deck.

17. What is the probability of consecutively picking two red cards from a standard deck, with replacement?

18. Calculate the probability of picking two black Aces from a standard deck consecutively, with replacement.

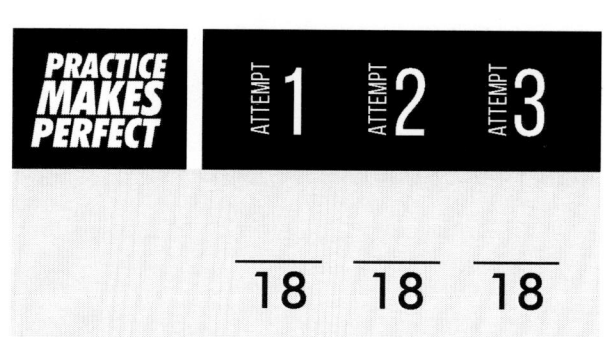

CHAPTER 30
CODING

You have just joined a secret agency as a codebreaker and must decrypt a set of equations as part of your induction training programme. There are three sets.

$A \odot B = A + B^2$
$A \cdot B = A^2 + B^2$

1. $3 \odot 5$

2. $3 \cdot 4$

3. $2 \times (3 \odot 4)$

4. $(5 \cdot 5) \div 2$

$A \triangleright B = 3A + B$
$A \triangleleft B = A + 3B$
$A \triangledown B = 3A + 3B$

5. $6 \triangleright 8$

6. $2 \triangleleft -7$

7. $(3 \triangleleft 4) \triangledown 12$

8. $(12 \triangleright 10) \triangledown (12 \triangleleft 15)$

A ✿ B = (A + B) ÷ 2
A ★ B = (A + B) ÷ 3
A ♥ B = (A + B) ÷ 4
A ☛ B = (A + B) ÷ 5

9. 4 ✿ -3

10. 11 ★ 16

11. 253 ♥ 367

12. 395 ☛ 360

USE ALL THE CODES FOR THE FOLLOWING QUESTIONS

13. (2 ◎ 3) ▶ (4 ♥ 12)

14. (4 ☛ 16)² − (2 · 4) × (6 ◀ -2)

15. (3 · 4) + (2 ◀ -7) × (6 ✿ 10)

16. (9 ✿ -8) + (10 ★ 5) × (8 ♥ 8)

17. (5 ◎ 10) ▶ (6 ♥ 14)

18. (3 ☛ 22)² − (4 · 5) × (2 ◀ 10)

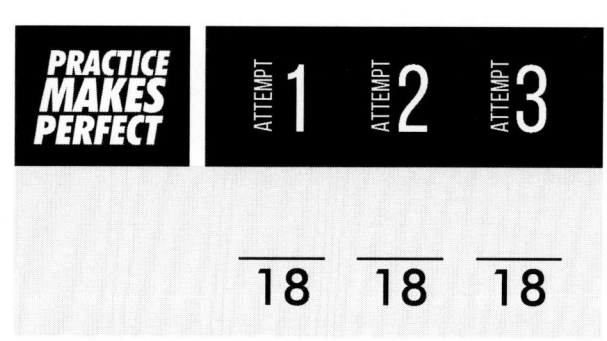

CHAPTER 31
MAPS

Complete the following questions on maps.

1. A scale on a map is 1:500. The length on the map is 10mm. Find the actual distance in a) mm, b) cm.

2. A scale on a map is 1:1000. The length on the map is 10cm. Find the actual distance in a) m, b) km.

3. A scale on a map is 1:10000. The length on the map is 7mm. Find the actual distance in a) mm, b) cm.

4. A scale on a map is 1:1000. The length on the map is 12cm. Find the actual distance in a) m, b) km.

5. A scale on a map is 1:10,000. The length on the map is 8cm. Find the actual distance in a) m b) km.

6. A scale on a map is 1:7000. The length on the map is 7cm. Find the actual distance in a) m, b) km.

7. A scale on a map is 1:8,000. The length on the map is 15cm. Find the actual distance in a) m, b) km.

8. A scale on a map is 1:50,000. The length on the map is 6mm. Find the actual distance in a) m, b) Km.

9. A scale on a map is 1:250,000. The length on the map is 8cm. Find the actual distance in a) m, b) km.

10. A scale on a map is 1:2,000,000. The length on the map is 9mm. Find the actual distance in a) m, b) km.

11. A scale on a map is 1:1,000,000. The length on the map is 8cm. Find the actual distance in a) m, b) km.

12. A scale on a map is 1:20,000,000. The length on the map is 5cm. Find the actual distance in a) m, b) km.

13. A scale on a map is 1:2000. The length on the map is 12mm. Find the actual distance in a) m, b) km.

14. A scale on a map is 1:500,000,000. The length on the map is 8mm. Find the actual distance in a) m, b) km.

15. A scale on a map is 1:10,000,000. The length on the map is 3cm. Find the actual distance in a) m, b) km.

16. A scale on a map is 1:25,000,000. The length on the map is 6cm. Find the actual distance in a) m, b) km.

17. A scale on a map is 1:50,000,000. The length on the map is 5cm. Find the actual distance in a) m, b) km.

18. A scale on a map is 1:100,000,000. The length on the map is 10cm. Find the actual distance in a) m, b) km.

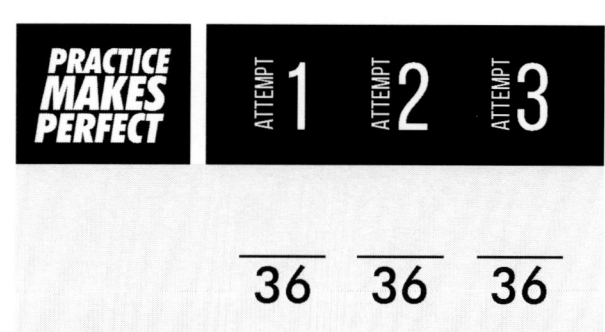

CHAPTER 31

MAPS
CONTINUED

Complete the following questions on maps.

1. The actual distance between Harrow and Pinner is 6km. If the scale on the map is 1:10000, what is the length on the map in cm?

2. The actual distance between Harrow and Pinner is 9km. If the scale on the map is 1:20000, what is the length on the map in cm?

3. The actual distance between Harrow and Hayes is 20km. If the scale on the map is 1:50000, what is the length on the map in cm?

4. The actual distance between Harrow and Hayes is 50km. If the scale on the map is 1:100000, what is the length on the map in cm?

5. The actual distance between Harrow and Hayes is 40km. If the scale on the map is 1:20000, what is the length on the map in cm?

6. The actual distance between two towns is 50km. If the scale on the map is 1:100000, what is the length on the map in cm?

7. The actual distance between two towns is 10km. If the scale on the map is 1:200000, what is the length on the map in cm?

8. The actual distance between two towns is 100km. If the scale on the map is 1:10000, what is the length on the map in cm?

9. The actual distance between two towns is 5km. If the scale on the map is 1:100000, what is the length on the map in cm?

10. The actual distance between two towns is 2km. If the scale on the map is 1:100000, what is the length on the map in mm?

11. The actual distance between two towns is 5km. If the scale on the map is 1:1000000, what is the length on the map in mm?

12. The actual distance between two towns is 80km. If the scale on the map is 1:20000, what is the length on the map in cm?

13. The actual distance between two towns is 5000km. If the scale on the map is 1:10000, what is the length on the map in cm?

14. The actual distance between two towns is 20km. If the scale on the map is 1:10000, what is the length on the map in cm?

15. The actual distance between two towns is 0.5km. If the scale on the map is 1:1000, what is the length on the map in cm?

16. The actual distance between two towns is 6.3km. If the scale on the map is 1:100000, what is the length on the map in cm?

17. The actual distance between two towns is 9.5km. If the scale on the map is 1:1000000, what is the length on the map in cm?

18. The actual distance between two towns is 0.04km. If the scale on the map is 1:10000, what is the length on the map in cm?

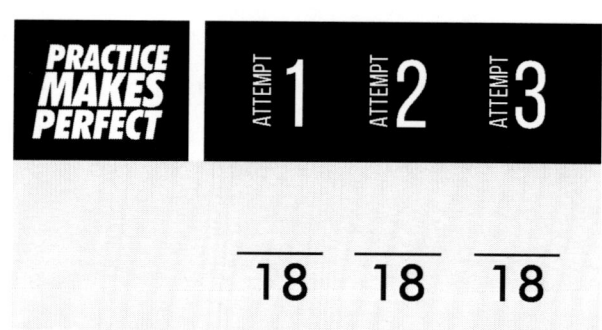

CHAPTER 32
METRIC UNITS

Complete the following questions on metric units.

1CM	1M	1KM	1G	1KG	1 TONNE	1CL	1L	1L
10MM	100CM	1000M	1000MG	1000G	1000KG	10ML	1000ML	100CL

1. Convert 70,000 centimetres into kilometres

2. Convert 0.08 tonnes into grams

3. Convert 34 centilitres into millilitres

4. Convert 2.6 kilograms into grams

5. Convert 0.5 metres into millimetres

6. Convert 40 grams into milligrams

7. Convert 310,000 millimetres into kilometres

8. Convert 9,080 millilitres into centilitres

9. Convert 700,000,000 milligrams into tonnes

10. Convert 655,000 centimetres into kilometres

11. Convert 786 centilitres into litres

12. Convert 0.0023 tonnes into milligrams

13. Convert 31,000 millilitres into centilitres

14. Convert 220,200 millimetres into kilometres

15. Convert 70,000 grams into kilograms

16. Convert 4.5 litres into centilitres

17. Convert 2,076 millimetres into centimetres

18. Convert 3 kilometre into centimetres

19. Convert 3 metres into millimetres

20. Convert 5 litres into millilitres

21. Convert 200 millimetres into centimetres

22. Convert 35 kilometre into centimetres

23. Convert 30 metres into millimetres

24. Convert 15 litres into millilitres

25. Convert 6,000 grams into kilograms

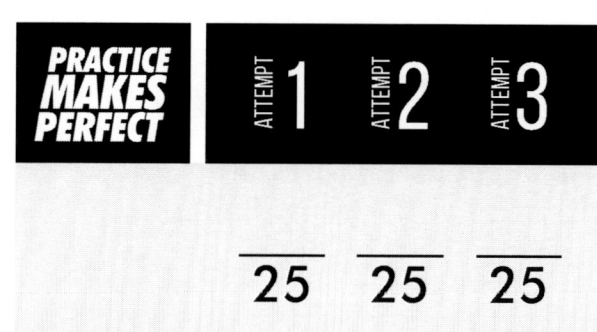

CHAPTER 33

IMPERIAL UNITS

Complete the following questions on imperial units.

1 FOOT	1 YARD	1 POUND (LB)	1 STONE	1 GALLON	1 TONNE	1 MILE
12 INCHES	3 FEET	16 OUNCES	14 LBS	8 PINTS	2240 LBS	1760 YARDS

1. Convert 13 yards to feet

2. Convert 4.5 stone to pounds

3. Convert 3 tonnes to pounds

4. Convert 80 feet to inches

5. Convert 5 pounds to ounces

6. Convert 300 gallons to pints

7. Convert 0.05 miles to yards

8. Convert 3,369 feet to yards

9. Convert 210 pounds to stone

10. Convert 4,480 pounds to tonnes

11. Convert 144 inches to feet

12. Convert 1,600 ounces to pounds

13. Convert 560 pints to gallons

14. Convert 8,800 yards to miles

15. Convert 0.0001 yards to feet

16. Convert 7 stone to pounds

17. Convert 0.00005 tonnes to pounds

18. Convert 3 feet into inches.

19. Convert 5 stone into ounces.

20. Convert 5 gallons into pints.

21. Convert 30 yards to feet

22. Convert 6.5 stone to pounds

23. Convert 5 tonnes to pounds

24. Convert 1200 feet to inches

25. Convert 16 pounds to ounces

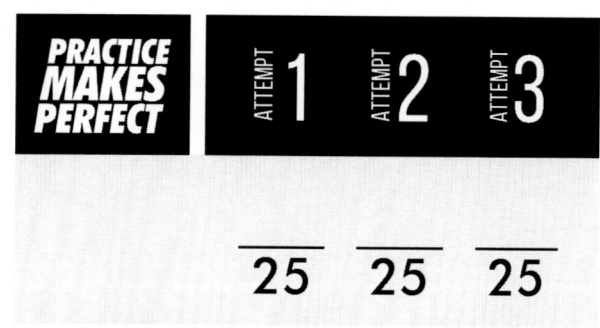

CHAPTER 34
CURRENCY CONVERSION

Complete the following questions on currency conversion.

| FR.1.2 | £1.00 | $1.25 | ¥134 | €1.1 |

1. Convert 12 Francs into Pound Sterling

2. Convert £0.50 Pound Sterling into Euros

3. Convert 268 Japanese Yen into US Dollars

4. Convert 1,100 Euros into Francs

5. Convert £3.00 Pound Sterling into Japanese Yen

6. Convert $12.50 US Dollars into Euros

7. Convert 24 Francs into US Dollars

8. Convert £0.25 Pound Sterling into Francs

9. Convert 33 Euros into Japanese Yen

10. Convert $12,500 US Dollars into Euros

11. Convert 1,440 Francs into Japanese Yen

12. Convert 1.34 Japanese Yen into Pound Sterling

13. Convert 0.55 Euros into Francs

14. Convert 48 Francs into Pound Sterling

15. Convert 5 Pound Sterling into Dollars

16. Convert 22 Euros into Pound Sterling

17. Convert 13400 Yen into Pound Sterling

18. Convert 2500 US Dollars into Pound Sterling

19. Convert 2400 Francs into Pound Sterling

20. Convert 1000 Pound Sterling into Dollars

21. Convert 0.01 Pound Sterling into Yen

22. Convert 100 US Dollars into Pound Sterling

23. Convert 120 Francs into Pound Sterling

24. Convert 10000 Pound Sterling into Dollars

25. Convert 0.20 Pound Sterling into Yen

CHAPTER 35
ESTIMATION

Estimate the answer to the following questions.

1. 10.011 x 9.602

2. 14.9789 x 10.2

3. 6.01 ÷ 0.19

4. 0.488 x 5.12

5. 5.007 x 0.3

6. 12.134 x 2.9

7. 0.0111 x 29.903

8. 6.857 ÷ 0.5

9. 4.031 x 0.2

10. 99.999 x 1.9121

11. 7.105 x 19.6

12. 3.9 ÷ 1.9

13. 18.020301 ÷ 8.97

14. 19.904 x 3.06

15. 8.0005 x 5

16. 2.867 ÷ 0.05

17. 0.49 x 8

18. 80.19 x 9.99

19. 5.987 ÷ 0.3

20. 0.404 ÷ 0.202

21. 19.819 x 5.07

22. 0.707 x 99

23. 34.8786 ÷ 7.055

24. 1009 ÷ 9.955

25. 19.6 x 41

PRACTICE MAKES PERFECT | ATTEMPT 1 | ATTEMPT 2 | ATTEMPT 3

—/25   —/25   —/25

CHAPTER 36
SEQUENCES

Find the missing numbers in the sequences below.

1. 20, ... , 10, 5 , 0

2. 13, 17 , 21, ...

3. 0, 10, 100, 1,000, ...

4. -2, 4, 10, ...

5. 48, 43, ... , 33, 28, 23

6. 110, 120, 130, ... , 150

7. 44, ... , 22, 11

8. 1, 1, 2, 3, 5, ...

9. 96, 85, 74, ... , 52

10. -1, ... , -11, -16

11. 4, 24, 44, 64, ...

12. ... , 12, 20, 28, 36

13. 2,000, ... , 20, 2, 0.2

14. 1.8, 3.8, ... , 7.8, 9.8

15. 90, 75, 60, ...

16. 32, 21, ... , -1

17. ... , 23, 33, 43

18. 1, 4, 9, 16, 25, ...

19. 1, 8, 27, 64, ...

20. 1, 3, 6, 10, 15, ...

21. 2, 5, 10, 17, 26, ...

22. 10, 20, 30, 40, ...

23. 5, 15, 35, 65, ...

24. 6, 36, 66, 96, ...

25. 100, 500, 900, 1300, ...

CHAPTER 36
SEQUENCES
Nᵀᴴ TERM

Work out the nᵗʰ term for the sequences below.

1. 8, 15, 22, 29, 36,

2. 56, 66, 76, 86, 96,

3. 100, 80, 60, 40, 20,

4. 13, 21, 29, 37, 45,

5. 18, 21, 24, 27, 30,

6. 1, 4, 9, 16, 25,

7. 20, 30, 40, 50, 60,

8. 70, 58, 46, 34, 22,

9. 0.5, 1.5, 2.5, 3.5, 4.5,

10. 9, 4, -1, -6, -11,

11. 4, 54, 104, 154, 204,

12. 11, 13, 15, 17, 19,

13. 0, 33, 66, 99,

14. 56, 45, 34, 23, 12,

15. 60, 45, 30, 15, 0,

16. -4, -8, -12, -16, -20,

17. 3, 5, 7, 9, 11,

18. 4, 7, 10, 13, 16,

19. 1, 8, 27, 64, 125,

20. 15, 25, 35, 45, 55,

21. 30, 50, 70, 90, 110

22. 1, 4, 7, 10, 13,

23. 9, 14, 19, 24, 29,

24. 6, 36, 66, 96,

25. 100, 500, 900, 1300,

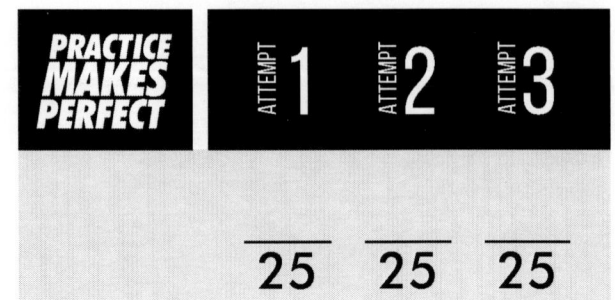

11+ MATHEMATICS 103

CHAPTER 37
CLOCKS

Complete the following questions on clocks.

1. Convert the time 17:37 into 12-hour format

2. Convert the time 03:20 into 12-hour format

3. Convert the time 01:10 into 12-hour format

4. Convert the time 19:55 into 12-hour format

5. Convert the time 13:46 into 12-hour format

6. Convert the time 00:00 into 12-hour format

7. Convert the time 09:09 into 12-hour format

8. Convert the time 18:14 into 12-hour format

9. Convert the time 12:00 into 12-hour format

10. Convert the time 11:53pm into 24-hour format

11. Convert the time 12:18pm into 24-hour format

12. Convert the time 7:36am into 24-hour format

13. Convert the time 9:09pm into 24-hour format

14. Convert the time 1:42pm into 24-hour format

15. Convert the time 6:00pm into 24-hour format

16. Convert the time 3:44am into 24-hour format

17. Convert the time 5:59am into 24-hour format

18. Convert the time 4:28pm into 24-hour format

19. Convert the time 2:44am into 24-hour format

20. Convert the time 8:59am into 24-hour format

21. Convert the time 3:28pm into 24-hour format

22. Convert the time 7:59am into 24-hour format

23. Convert the time 7:52am into 24-hour format

24. Convert the time 6:59pm into 24-hour format

25. Convert the time 11:59am into 24-hour format

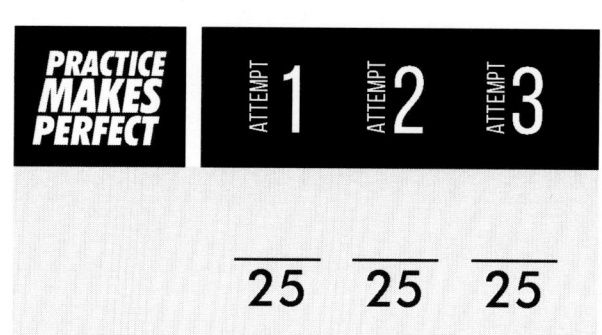

CHAPTER 37

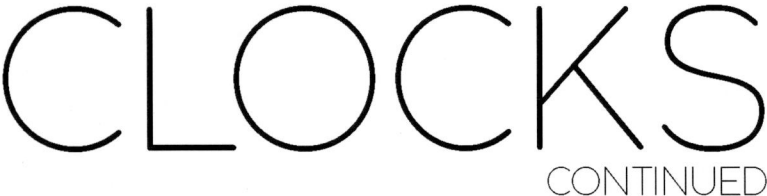
CONTINUED

Work out how many hours and minutes are between the times below.

1. 06:23 to 13:51?

2. Monday 06:10 to Wednesday 13:30?

3. 12:46 to 19:19?

4. Saturday 03:20 to Sunday 18:44?

5. 19:09 to 00:15?

6. Thursday 14:12 to Saturday 15:21?

7. 08:18 to 18:08?

8. Tuesday 21:35 to Friday 00:00?

9. 13:31 to 15:51?

10. Sunday 04:56 to Monday 12:20?

11. 12:24 to 17:01?

12. Friday 01:10 to Monday 10:01?

13. 09:18 to 14:05?

14. Wednesday 00:00 to Friday 00:00?

15. 01:31 to 18:27?

16. Monday 19:45 to Thursday 20:50?

17. 10:52 to 16:10?

18. Sunday 03:30 to Tuesday 00:00?

19. 02:36 to 19:27?

20. 13:45 to 19:55?

21. 03:56 to 03:59?

22. 11:12 to 14:55?

23. 08:35 to 11:26?

24. 13:45 to 23:21?

25. Wednesday 03:55 to Friday 19:56?

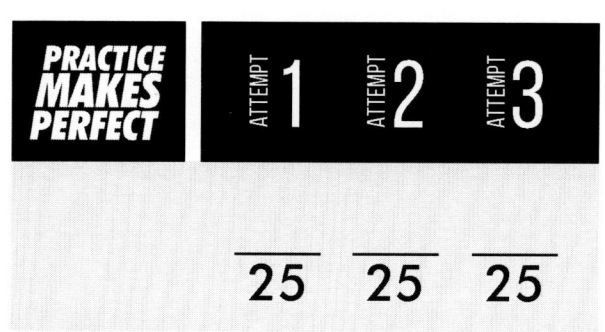

CHAPTER 37

CLOCKS
CONTINUED

Work out the following questions.

1. Calculate the number of degrees between the minute hand and the hour hand of a standard clock at 13:30.

2. Calculate the number of degrees between the minute hand and the hour hand of a standard clock at 04:20.

3. Calculate the number of degrees between the minute hand and hour hand of a standard clock at 00:00.

4. Calculate the number of degrees between the minute hand and hour hand of a standard clock at 20:00.

5. Calculate the number of degrees between the minute hand and hour hand of a standard clock at 02:00.

6. Calculate the number of degrees between the minute hand and hour hand of a standard clock at 18:20.

7. Calculate the number of degrees between the minute hand and hour hand of a standard clock at 03:30.

8. Calculate the number of degrees between the minute hand and hour hand of a standard clock at 19:30.

9. Calculate the number of degrees between the minute hand and hour hand of a standard clock at 09:00.

10. Calculate the number of degrees between the minute hand and hour hand of a standard clock at 15:20.

11. Calculate the number of degrees between the minute hand and hour hand of a standard clock at 16:20.

12. Calculate the number of degrees between the minute hand and hour hand of a standard clock at 18:30.

13. Calculate the number of degrees between the minute hand and hour hand of a standard clock at 20:20.

14. Calculate the number of degrees between the minute hand and hour hand of a standard clock at 06:00.

15. Calculate the number of degrees between the minute hand and hour hand of a standard clock at 13:00.

16. Calculate the number of degrees between the minute hand and hour hand of a standard clock at 19:00.

17. Calculate the number of degrees between the minute hand and hour hand of a standard clock at 17:30.

18. Calculate the number of degrees between the minute hand and hour hand of a standard clock at 03:00.

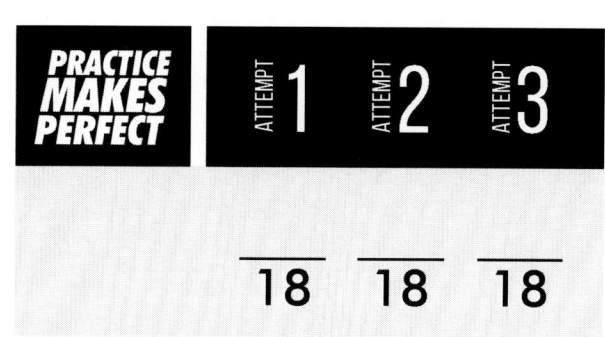

CHAPTER 38
COORDINATES

Answer the questions below, using the grid below.

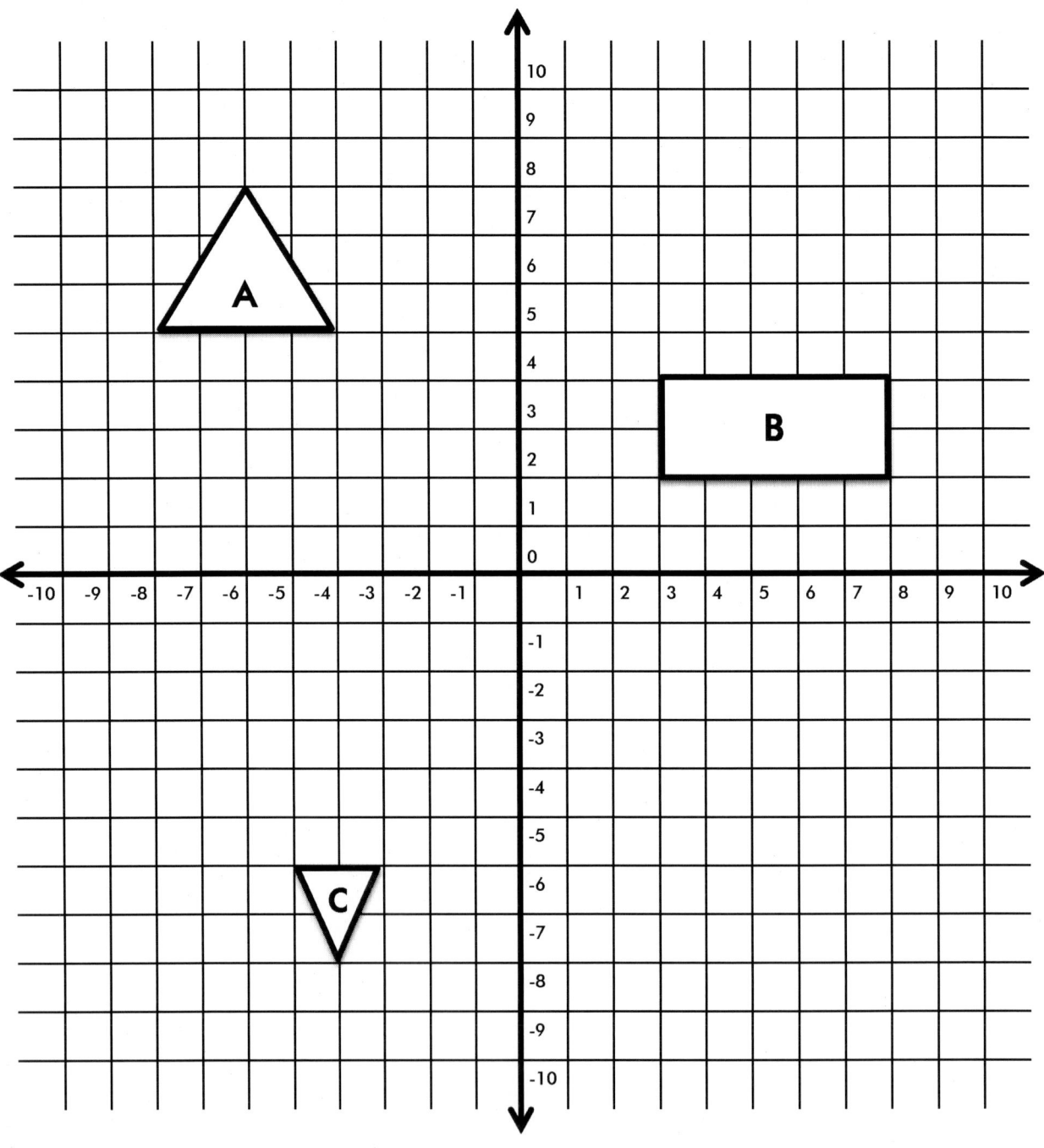

1. Translate the shape labelled 'A' by (3, -1) and state the coordinates of the new shape, now labelled 'D'

2. Reflect the shape labelled 'B' in the x-axis, and state the coordinates of the new shape, now labelled 'E'

3. Translate the shape labelled 'C' by (-5, 1) and state the coordinates of the new shape, now labelled 'F'

4. Translate the shape labelled 'E' by (2, 2) and state the coordinates of the new shape, now labelled 'G'

5. Reflect the shape labelled 'D' in the y-axis and state the coordinates of the new shape, now labelled 'H'

6. Calculate the translation that would be required to map the shape labelled 'G' onto the shape labelled 'B'

7. Translate the shape labelled 'H' by (3, -2) and state the coordinates of the new shape, now labelled 'I'

8. Calculate the transformation that would be required to map the shape labelled 'I' onto the shape labelled 'A'

9. Reflect the shape labelled 'C' in the y-axis and state the coordinates of the new shape

10. Translate the shape labelled 'B' by (-2, 4) and state the coordinates of the new shape

CHAPTER 39
PROBLEM SOLVING

Work out the following questions.

1. Harry is 4 years older than Tom. The sum of their ages is 88.
a. What is Harry's age?
b. What is Tom's age?

2. Harry is 10 years older than Tom. The sum of their ages is 62.
a. What is Harry's age?
b. What is Tom's age?

3. Harry is half as old as Tom. The sum of their ages is 90.
a. What is Harry's age?
b. What is Tom's age?

4. My age is currently a multiple of 7, next year it will be a multiple of 5. I am older than 20 but less than 81. What is my age?

5. In four years' time, Megan will be twice as old as she was 4 years ago. What is her current age?

6. 5 years ago, the combined ages of three children is 33. What is their combined age in 3 years' time?

7. One third of the animals on a farm are pigs, the rest are goats. There are twelve more goats than pigs. How many animals are there altogether on the farm?

8. One third of the animals on a farm are pigs, the rest are goats. There are 200 more goats than pigs. How many animals are there altogether on the farm?

9. If Sean is the 50th fastest and slowest runner in her school, how many students are there in her school?

10. What weighs more – A kilogram of oranges or a kilogram of feathers?

11. The average age of six students in a class is 15. When the teacher is included the average age increases to 20. How old is the teacher?

12. The average age of five students in a class is 16. When the teacher is included the average age increases to 25. How old is the teacher?

13. An alloy is made by mixing Metal A and Metal B in the ratio 2:3. The cost of Metal A is £20/kg and Metal B is £60/kg. What is the cost of making 5kg of alloy?

14. A stone is made by mixing Metal A and Metal B in the ratio 2:3. The cost of Metal A is £10/kg and Metal B is £30/kg. What is the cost of making 0.5kg of alloy?

15. What is the smallest number of coins required to make £1.19?

16. What is the smallest number of coins required to make £2.21?

17. When freezing, water increases its volume by 1/11. By what part of its volume will ice decrease when it melts and turns back into water?

18. When freezing, water increases its volume by 1/15. By what part of its volume will ice decrease when it melts and turns back into water?

19. One car was leaving Plymouth at the same time a motorbike left London. The car was travelling at 40 mph and the motorbike was travelling at 30 mph. When the two vehicles meet, the car had done 20 miles more than the motorbike.

a. What is the distance from Plymouth to London?
b. How many minutes in total is the journey for the car to travel from Plymouth to London?
c. When the vehicles meet, were they closer to London or Plymouth?

20. A t-shirt cost £60 after the sales. What was the original price if it was reduced by 40%?

21. A jumper cost £100 after the sales. What was the original price if it was reduced by 80%?

22. Find the sum of all the numbers between 0 and 10?

23. Find the sum of all the numbers between 0 and 100?

24. Find the sum of all the numbers between 0 and 1000?

25. Ben used an old calculator to find out that 15 x 691 = 12347. Using this equation work out:
a. 150 x 6910
b. 0.15 x 691
c. 12347 ÷ 6.91
d. 12347 ÷ 691

26. A man invests £1000 in to a savings account. The interest rate is 10% yearly.
a. How much money does he have in his account after one year?
b. How much money does he have in his account after two years?
c. How much money does he have in his account after three years?

27. Write 48 as a product of its prime factors.

28. Write 36 as a product of its prime factors.

29. During World War 2 there was enough food to last 9000 people for 4800 days. How long would the food last if there were 36000 people?

30. During the Cold War there was enough food to last 4500 people for 1800 days. How long would the food last if there were 4000 people?

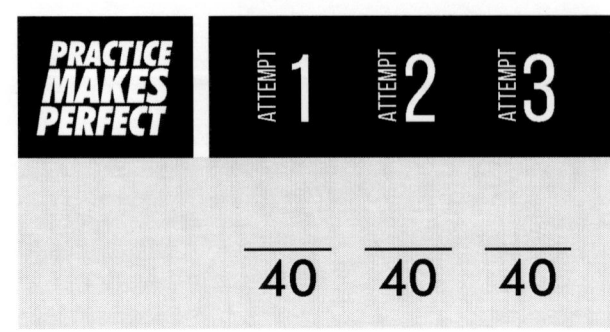

CHAPTER 40
BAR CHARTS

Answer the following questions on the favourite subjects of all the pupils in Year 7.

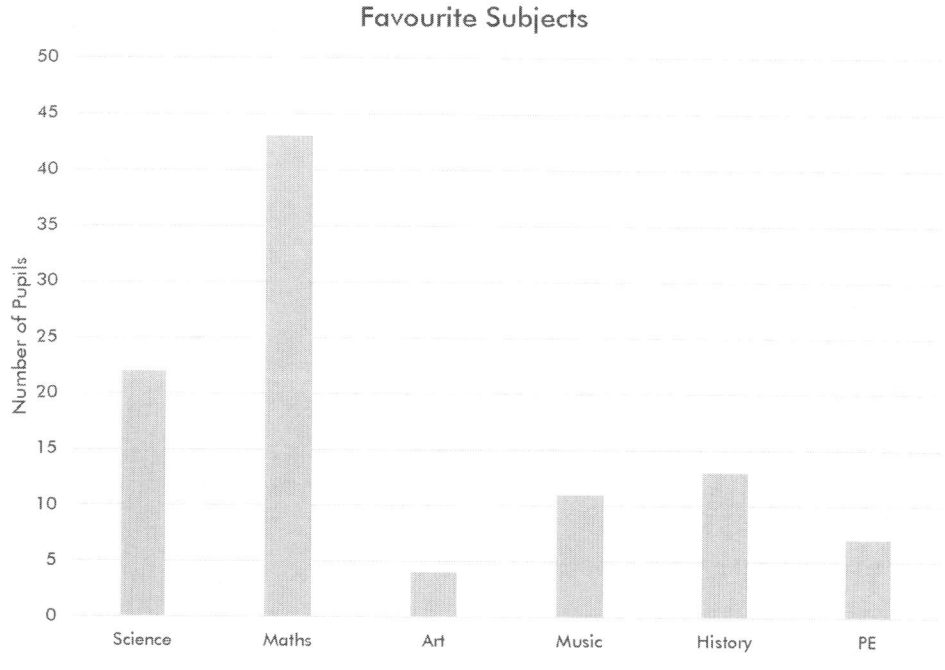

1. How many pupils prefer Maths over History?

2. How many pupils prefer Science or Music?

3. How many pupils are there in total?

4. What fraction of pupils do not prefer Science or Maths?

5. How many pupils prefer History over PE?

6. What percentage of pupils prefer Art?

7. How many pupils prefer Music or Maths?

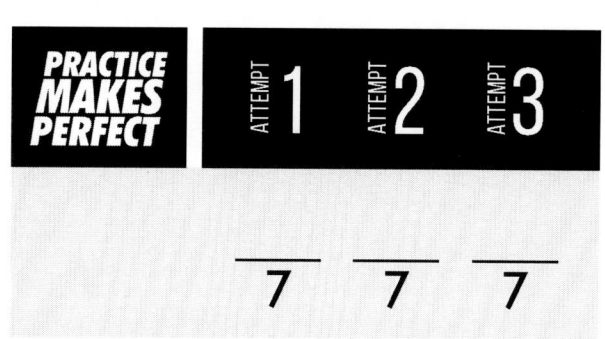

CHAPTER 41
PIE CHARTS

Answer the following questions on the school journeys of Year 7, which consists of 80 pupils.

1. How many pupils travel to school by car?

2. What fraction of the pupils go to school by bus?

3. How many pupils do not travel to school by cycling?

4. What is the difference between the number of pupils who go to school by bus, compared to those who walk?

5. What percentage of pupils walk to school?

6. How many of the pupils go to school on a four-wheeled vehicle?

7. What fraction of the pupils do not travel to school by car?

School Journey

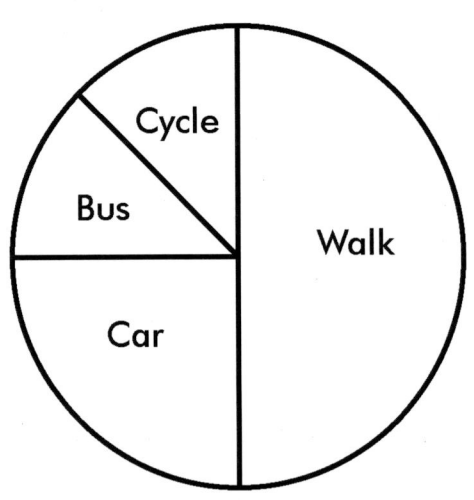

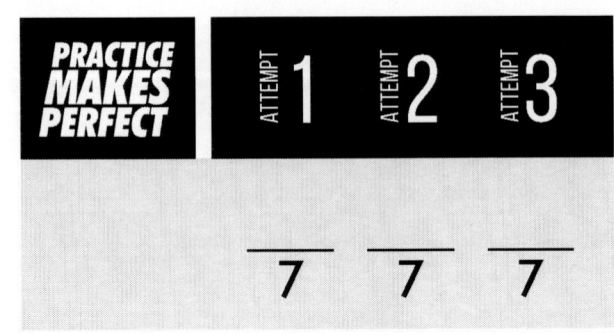

PIE CHARTS
CHAPTER 41
CONTINUED

Answer the following questions on the favourite colours of the 90 pupils in Year 3.

Favourite Colours

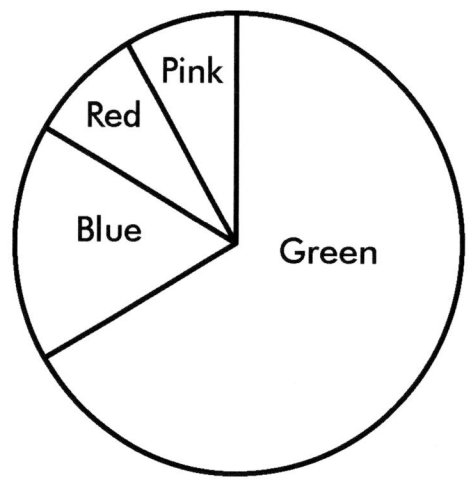

1. What fraction of the pupils prefer the colour green?

2. How many of the pupils prefer the colour blue?

3. What fraction of pupils prefer the colour blue, red or pink?

4. How many pupils prefer green or blue in total?

5. What fraction of pupils prefer blue?

6. What is the difference in the number of pupils that prefer green, compared to the number of pupils that prefer blue?

7. How many of the pupils do not prefer the colour green?

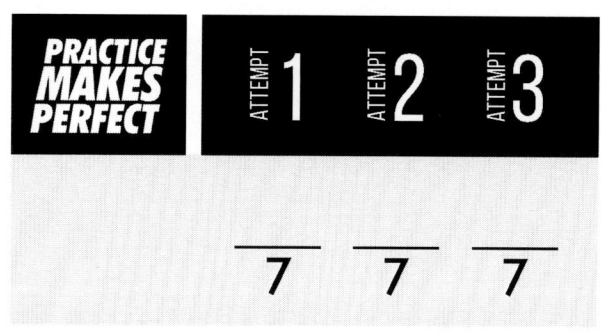

CHAPTER 42
TRAIN TIMETABLE

Complete the following questions using the train timetable below.

LOCATION	A	B	C	D
LONDON	06:40	07:10	06:40	06:55
READING	07:10	07:40	07:10	07:25
BRISTOL	08:35	08:10	07:25	07:45
EXETER	09:45	08:30	08:40	08:30
PLYMOUTH	10:50	09:15	09:55	09:10
PENZANCE	11:10	09:40	10:30	09:50

1. If Ben takes train A, what time will he reach Bristol?

2. Which train leaves last from London?

3. Which train is the slowest from London to Penzance?

4. Which train is the fastest from London to Penzance?

5. How long in minutes does train C take from London to Penzance?

6. How long in minutes does train B take from London to Penzance?

7. Which train is the fastest from Bristol to Penzance?

8. To get to Penzance by 10:00, what is the latest time you can leave Bristol?

9. Which train arrives at Plymouth the earliest?

10. Which train is the fastest between Bristol and Exeter?

11. What time must Kate take train A if she is travelling from Reading?

12. How long does train A take from London to Penzance?

13. Sharon needs to be at Bristol station at 07:35, what train must she take?

14. Tom needs to be at Plymouth by 09:12. Which train should he take?

15. Bob gets to Reading station at 07:10, which train will get him to Plymouth as soon as possible?

CHAPTER 43

FREQUENCY TABLE

The frequency table below shows the amount of goals scored by players during the last 5 football matches between Manchester United and Barcelona. Use the table to answer the questions below.

TEAM	PLAYER	MATCH 1	MATCH 2	MATCH 3	MATCH 4	MATCH 5
MANCHESTER UNITED	RASHFORD	2	1	1	1	3
MANCHESTER UNITED	MARTIAL	0	1	0	0	3
MANCHESTER UNITED	GREENWOOD	0	2	1	0	0
BARCELONA	MESSI	1	0	5	1	2
BARCELONA	SUAREZ	0	2	0	2	0
BARCELONA	NEYMAR	1	0	0	1	3

1. How many goals were scored in match 3?

2. Which team won match 4?

3. Which player scored the most goals in total?

4. Which player scored in all five games?

5. How many games did Manchester United win?

6. How many goals did Martial score in total?

7. Who scored the most goals for Manchester United in total?

8. What percentage of goals did Messi score for Barcelona?

9. How many goals did Barcelona score in total?

10. How many goals did Manchester United score in total?

11. What is the simplified ratio of Manchester United to Barcelona goals in total?

12. What fraction of goals did Rashford score out of the total number of goals in Match 1?

13. Martial and Greenwood played in 4 matches, Neymar played in 3 matches and Suarez played in 2 matches. Everyone else played all 5 games. Who has the highest goals to game ratio?

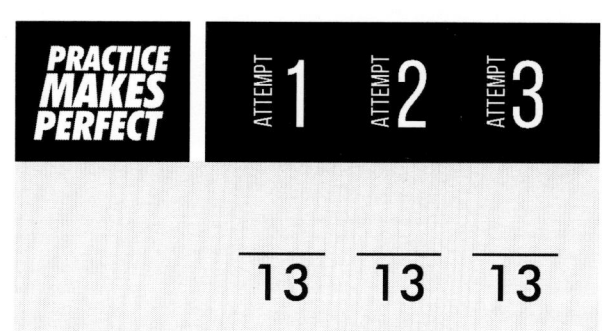

CHAPTER 44
LINE SYMMETRY

Find the number of lines of symmetry of the following shapes.

1)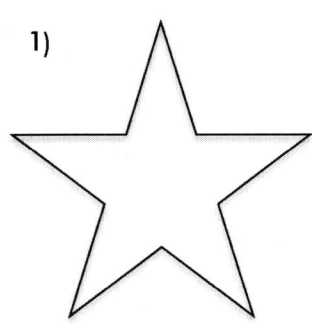

2)

3)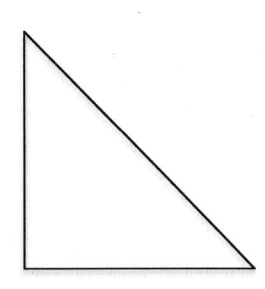

4)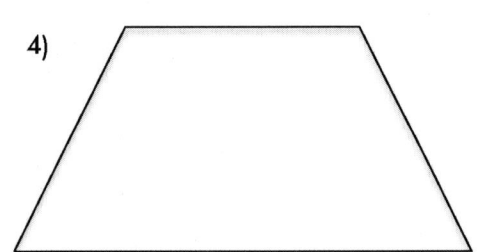

5)

6)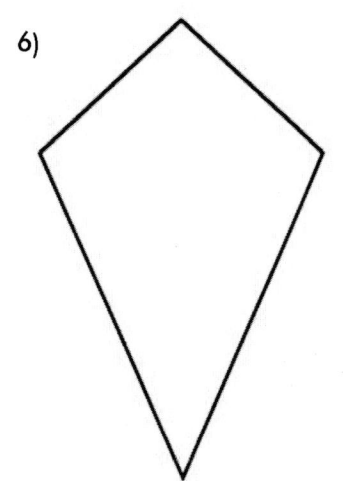

7)

8)

ROTATIONAL SYMMETRY

Determine whether the following shapes possess rotational symmetry and if so, to what order?

1)

2)

3)

4)

5)

6)

7)

8)

PRACTICE MAKES PERFECT

ATTEMPT 1	ATTEMPT 2	ATTEMPT 3
___ / 8	___ / 8	___ / 8

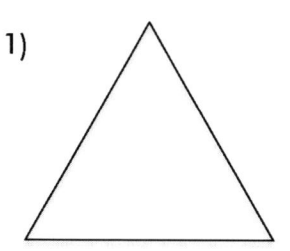

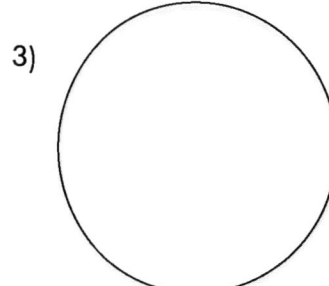

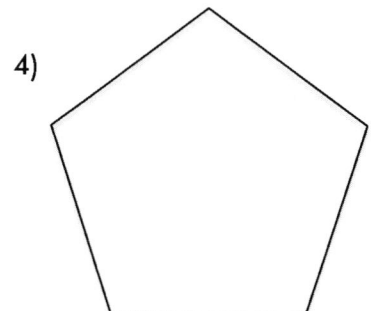

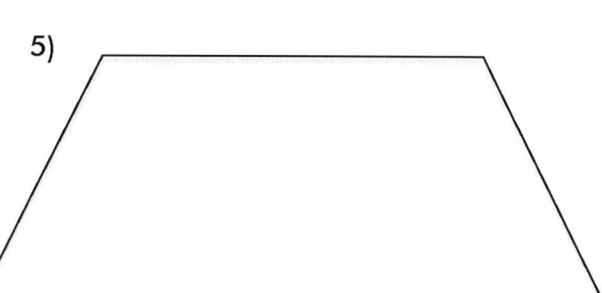

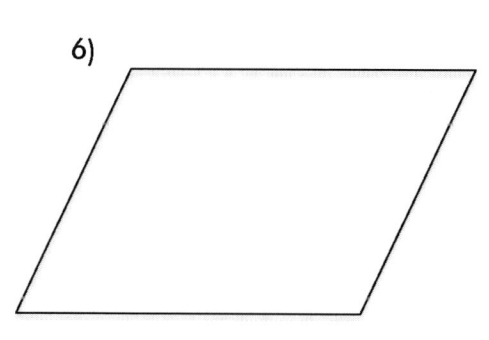

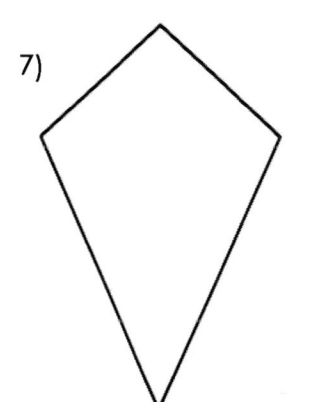

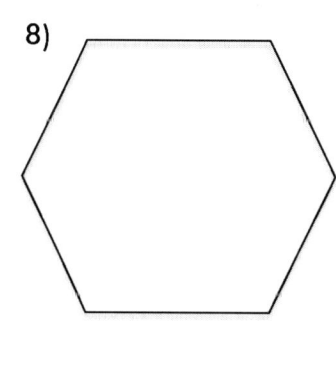

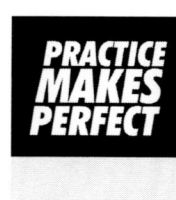

CHAPTER 46
SPEED, DISTANCE, TIME

Work out the following questions.

1. A car travels at 30 miles per hour for 2 hours. How far does it travel?

2. A bike travels at 50 miles per hour for 4 hours. How far does it travel?

3. A lorry travels at 20 miles per hour for 6 hours. How far does it travel?

4. A boy runs at 10 m/s for 20 seconds. How many metres does he run?

5. A cheetah runs at 30m/s for 60 seconds. How many kilometres does it run?

6. A plane flew 800 kilometres in 4 hours. What was its speed in kilometre/hour?

7. A helicopter flew 1200 miles in 12 hours. What was its speed in miles/hour?

8. A girl ran a 100 metre race in 12 seconds. What was her speed in metres/second?

9. A tortoise moved 1 metre in 100 seconds. What was its speed in metres/second?

10. An old man walked 5 miles in 4 hours. What was his speed in miles/hour?

11. How long did it take Usain Bolt to run 100 metres at a speed of 10m/s?

12. How long did it take a boy to run 5000 metres at a speed of 2.5m/s?

13. How long did it take a speedboat to travel 100 kilometres at a speed of 12.5km/hr?

14. How long did it take a plane to travel 2000 kilometres at a speed of 800km/hr?

15. How long did it take a bullet to travel 80 metres at a speed of 120m/s?

16. Harry finished faster than Tom in a 200 metre race by 5 seconds. If it took Harry 20 seconds to finish the race:

    a. What speed was Harry running at in metres/ second?

    b. What speed was Tom running at in metres/ second?

17. A car was leaving Exeter at the same time a motorbike left Manchester. The car was travelling at 80mph and the motorbike was travelling at 60mph. When the two vehicles meet, the car had done 60 miles more than the motorbike.

    a. What is the distance from Exeter to Manchester?

    b. How many minutes in total does it take the car to reach Manchester from Exeter?

    c. When the vehicles meet, were they closer to Manchester or Exeter?

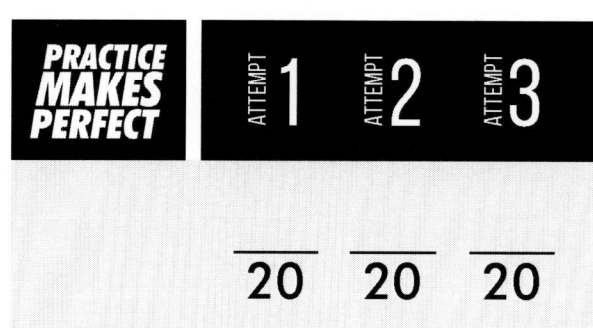

ANSWERS

ANSWERS

Page 6

1. 58	10. 107	19. 3685
2. 79	11. 449	20. 3191
3. 120	12. 605	21. 58023
4. 123	13. 709	22. 133032
5. 139	14. 365	23. 124461
6. 122	15. 401	24. 186200
7. 149	16. 9129	25. 78519
8. 155	17. 5205	
9. 147	18. 6374	

Page 7

1. 18	10. 61	19. 3689
2. 53	11. 341	20. 987
3. 42	12. 129	21. 42889
4. 47	13. 561	22. 55436
5. 13	14. 669	23. 24387
6. 64	15. 471	24. 30867
7. 41	16. 1061	25. 37882
8. 49	17. 3029	
9. 13	18. 4626	

Page 8

1. 30	10. 98	19. 728
2. 32	11. 120	20. 810
3. 63	12. 160	21. 1015
4. 48	13. 121	22. 1080
5. 45	14. 156	23. 1763
6. 104	15. 182	24. 1363
7. 44	16. 240	25. 7448
8. 60	17. 306	
9. 78	18. 575	

Page 9

1. 2	10. 13	19. 43
2. 5	11. 15	20. 21
3. 5	12. 25	21. 25
4. 5	13. 10	22. 48.75
5. 7	14. 10	23. 15.75
6. 2	15. 95	24. 61
7. 15	16. 31	25. 409
8. 11	17. 102	
9. 12	18. 62	

Page 10

1. 1055	10. 121	19. 39206
2. 24	11. 612	20. 120
3. 151	12. 164	21. 1311
4. 980	13. 14	22. 492
5. 187	14. 893	23. 17
6. 111	15. 243	24. 212.8
7. 2424	16. 784	25. 1810.67
8. 62	17. 2604	
9. 656	18. 132	

Page 11

1. 50	14. 9
2. 700	15. 60
3. 8000	16. 2300
4. 20 000	17. 1010
5. 4	18. 123400
6. 60	19. 12389000
7. 900	20. 987900000
8. 7000	21. 1030
9. 140	22. 1050
10. 1800	23. 2303500
11. 29000	24. 35300
12. 450 000	25. 234.5
13. 0.5	

Page 12

1. 0.1	18. 0.0106
2. 0.02	19. 0.010009
3. 0.005	20. 0.012009
4. 0.0006	21. 12.34
5. 0.03	22. 23.456
6. 0.004	23. 54.32
7. 0.0007	24. 0.435
8. 0.00009	25. 5.43
9. 1.2	
10. 0.15	
11. 0.052	
12. 0.0234	
13. 0.003	
14. 0.0006	
15. 0.000008	
16. 0.0000009	
17. 0.103	

Page 13

Prime Numbers:
2 3 5 7 11 13 17
19 23 29 31 37
41 43 47 53 59
61 67 71 73 79
83 89 97 101 103
107 109 113 127
131 137 139

Square Numbers:
1 4 9 16 25 36 49
64 81 100 121

Cube Numbers:
1 8 27 64 125

Page 14

1. LCM=10, HCF=5	14. LCM=28, HCF=7
2. LCM=20, HCF=2	15. LCM=60, HCF=10
3. LCM=12, HCF=3	16. LCM=60, HCF=3
4. LCM=30, HCF=3	17. LCM=240, HCF=2
5. LCM=60, HCF=2	18. LCM=90, HCF=6
6. LCM=18, HCF=9	19. LCM=150, HCF=5
7. LCM=50, HCF=5	20. LCM=200, HCF=10
8. LCM=30, HCF=5	21. LCM=150, HCF=10
9. LCM=20, HCF=10	22. LCM=100, HCF=50
10. LCM=27, HCF=9	23. LCM=600, HCF=50
11. LCM=120, HCF=4	24. LCM=140, HCF=2
12. LCM=72, HCF=6	25. LCM=50, HCF=25
13. LCM=42, HCF=7	

ANSWERS

Page 15

Question	Mean	Mode	Median	Range
1.	4	4	4	2
2.	4	2	3	7
3.	6	6	6	10
4.	6	6	6	7
5.	6	6	6	10
6.	5	5	5	0
7.	10	10	10	14
8.	12	12	12	4
9.	10	10	10	14
10.	40	50	45	30
11.	1.6	4	4	6
12.	-2.4	-2	-2	3
13.	0	3	0	11
14.	-10	-12	-12	8
15.	15	11	11	30
16.	14	12	13.5	10
17.	5	6	5.5	3
18.	4	7	3	6
19.	6	5	5	6
20.	5	2	4	8
21.	-3	-3	-3	5
22.	-8	-11	-9	10
23.	10	10	10	0
24.	8	8	8	7
25.	2	2	2	2

Page 16

1. 2:3
2. 2:3
3. 5:6
4. 1:2
5. 3:5
6. 3:5
7. 1:3
8. 4:5
9. 1:3
10. 1:4
11. 7:10
12. 1:3
13. 1:4
14. 1:3
15. 1:4
16. 5:18
17. 1:3
18. 4:5
19. 3:10
20. 1:2
21. 1:2
22. 3:4
23. 1:5
24. 2:25
25. 1:3

Page 17

1. 2:8
2. 1:9
3. 8:12
4. 20:10
5. 12:18
6. 10:40
7. 10:15
8. 2:16
9. 40:60
10. 45:105
11. 80:40
12. 30:90
13. 32:128
14. 2:8
15. 4:16
16. 6:24
17. 20:30
18. 20:80
19. 20:60
20. 200:800
21. 900:1100
22. 1000:4000
23. 50:250
24. 40:60
25. 7:28

Page 18

1. T= 20 V=10
2. T= 40 V=20
3. T= 60 V=30
4. T= 120 V=60
5. T= 2400 V=1200
6. T= 100 V=200
7. T= 200 V=400
8. T= 400 V=800
9. T= 30 V=20
10. T= 60 V=40
11. T= 120 V=80
12. T= 300 V=200
13. T= 500 V=300
14. T= 4 P=2 S=1
15. T= 40 P=20 S=10
16. T= 120 P=60 S=30
17. T= 400 P=200 S=100
18. T= 800 P=400 S=200
19. T= 60 P=20 S=40
20. T= 120 P=40 S=80
21. T= 240 P=80 S=160
22. T= 480 P=160 S=320
23. T= 48 P=16 S=32
24. T=120 P=60 H=120
25. T=240 P=120 H=240

Page 20

1. 6
1b. 18
2. 10
2b. 25
3. 12
3b. 28
4. 8
4b. 18
5. 6
5b. 24
6. 150
6b. 200
6c. 360
7. 200
7b. 300
7c. 520
8. 100
8b. 700
8c. 1400
9. 10
9b. 2
9c. 20
10. 30
10b. 25
10c. 75

Page 22

1. £16
2. £60
3. £620
4. 250
5. 480
6. 320
7. £200
8. £250
9. £112
10. £50
11. £18
12. £6
13. £2
14. £8
15. £36.60
16. £1.96
17. £7.20
18. £1
19. 200
20. 400
21. 800km
22. 160km
23. 320km
24. 80km
25. 240km

Page 24

1. 3
2. 3
3. 8
4. 10
5. 2
6. 6
7. 12
8. 1.5
9. 6
10. 3
11. 12
12. 1.5
13. 12
14. 6

Page 26

1. 0.25
2. 25
3. 0.75
4. 75
5. 1/3
6. 0.33
7. 2/3
8. 0.67
9. 0.2
10. 20
11. 0.4
12. 40
13. 0.6
14. 60
15. 1/5
16. 80
17. 0.125
18. 12.5
19. 0.375
20. 37.5
21. 0.625
22. 62.5
23. 7/8
24. 0.875
25. 0.1
26. 10
27. 0.3
28. 30
29. 0.7
30. 70
31. 9/10
32. 90
33. 0.05
34. 5
35. 0.35
36. 35
37. 0.65
38. 65
39. 0.26
40. 26
41. 0.39
42. 39

ANSWERS

Page 27
1. $1\tfrac{1}{2}$
2. $\tfrac{25}{4}$
3. $\tfrac{5}{2}$
4. $\tfrac{17}{4}$
5. $\tfrac{21}{2}$
6. $\tfrac{19}{6}$
7. $\tfrac{17}{2}$
8. $\tfrac{28}{3}$
9. $\tfrac{23}{2}$
10. $\tfrac{49}{8}$
11. $\tfrac{29}{4}$
12. $\tfrac{57}{7}$
13. $\tfrac{9}{2}$
14. $\tfrac{19}{3}$
15. $\tfrac{25}{4}$
16. $\tfrac{28}{3}$
17. $\tfrac{9}{4}$
18. $\tfrac{5}{4}$
19. $\tfrac{6}{5}$
20. $\tfrac{16}{5}$
21. $\tfrac{33}{8}$
22. $\tfrac{16}{5}$
23. $\tfrac{9}{5}$
24. $\tfrac{7}{6}$
25. $\tfrac{7}{3}$

Page 28
1. $2\tfrac{4}{5}$
2. $2\tfrac{1}{2}$
3. $10\tfrac{1}{2}$
4. $9\tfrac{1}{3}$
5. $6\tfrac{1}{8}$
6. $7\tfrac{5}{7}$
7. $6\tfrac{1}{3}$
8. $6\tfrac{7}{9}$
9. $4\tfrac{2}{5}$
10. $2\tfrac{2}{3}$
11. $2\tfrac{3}{4}$
12. $5\tfrac{1}{3}$
13. $7\tfrac{1}{4}$
14. $6\tfrac{1}{3}$
15. $9\tfrac{1}{3}$
16. $12\tfrac{1}{2}$
17. $3\tfrac{2}{3}$
18. $4\tfrac{1}{2}$
19. $1\tfrac{1}{2}$
20. $6\tfrac{2}{3}$
21. $5\tfrac{2}{3}$
22. $17\tfrac{1}{2}$
23. $10\tfrac{1}{3}$
24. $14\tfrac{1}{2}$
25. $1\tfrac{1}{5}$

Page 29
1. $\tfrac{3}{4}$
2. $\tfrac{5}{6}$
3. $\tfrac{9}{10}$
4. $\tfrac{1}{2}$
5. $\tfrac{7}{8}$
6. $\tfrac{3}{4}$
7. $\tfrac{3}{4}$
8. $\tfrac{3}{5}$
9. $\tfrac{2}{9}$
10. $\tfrac{11}{12}$
11. $\tfrac{11}{14}$
12. $\tfrac{17}{21}$
13. $\tfrac{9}{10}$
14. $\tfrac{7}{9}$
15. $\tfrac{4}{5}$
16. $\tfrac{5}{6}$
17. $\tfrac{10}{11}$
18. $\tfrac{5}{6}$
19. 1
20. $\tfrac{4}{5}$
21. $\tfrac{8}{9}$
22. $\tfrac{2}{5}$
23. $\tfrac{7}{9}$
24. $\tfrac{8}{11}$
25. $\tfrac{5}{7}$

Page 30
1. $\tfrac{4}{7}$
2. $\tfrac{7}{10}$
3. $\tfrac{7}{12}$
4. $\tfrac{1}{12}$
5. $\tfrac{1}{2}$
6. $\tfrac{1}{3}$
7. $\tfrac{4}{9}$
8. $\tfrac{3}{10}$
9. $\tfrac{1}{2}$
10. $\tfrac{7}{11}$
11. $\tfrac{1}{12}$
12. $\tfrac{7}{20}$
13. $\tfrac{4}{11}$
14. $\tfrac{1}{6}$
15. $\tfrac{3}{10}$
16. $\tfrac{3}{11}$
17. $\tfrac{5}{12}$
18. $\tfrac{4}{25}$
19. $\tfrac{3}{13}$
20. $\tfrac{7}{11}$
21. $\tfrac{1}{2}$
22. $\tfrac{2}{5}$
23. $\tfrac{4}{11}$
24. $\tfrac{1}{4}$
25. $\tfrac{7}{25}$

Page 31
1. $1\tfrac{3}{20}$
2. $3\tfrac{5}{14}$
3. $2\tfrac{3}{35}$
4. $1\tfrac{1}{2}$
5. $2\tfrac{5}{6}$
6. $3\tfrac{1}{3}$
7. $1\tfrac{9}{14}$
8. $1\tfrac{3}{4}$
9. $\tfrac{5}{6}$
10. $1\tfrac{2}{15}$
11. $2\tfrac{1}{14}$
12. $3\tfrac{5}{14}$
13. 1
14. $1\tfrac{1}{5}$
15. $1\tfrac{5}{12}$
16. $1\tfrac{1}{2}$
17. $\tfrac{11}{12}$
18. $\tfrac{18}{25}$
19. $\tfrac{7}{8}$
20. $\tfrac{4}{5}$
21. $1\tfrac{1}{28}$
22. $\tfrac{8}{9}$
23. $1\tfrac{1}{6}$
24. $1\tfrac{21}{25}$
25. $\tfrac{17}{24}$

Page 32
1. $\tfrac{1}{10}$
2. $\tfrac{1}{21}$
3. $\tfrac{3}{10}$
4. $\tfrac{1}{12}$
5. $\tfrac{1}{12}$
6. $\tfrac{4}{21}$
7. $\tfrac{19}{30}$
8. $\tfrac{7}{36}$
9. $\tfrac{1}{3}$
10. $\tfrac{17}{30}$
11. $\tfrac{1}{3}$
12. $\tfrac{1}{24}$
13. $\tfrac{2}{15}$
14. $\tfrac{5}{24}$
15. $\tfrac{3}{10}$
16. $\tfrac{7}{15}$
17. $\tfrac{1}{2}$
18. $\tfrac{3}{14}$
19. $\tfrac{5}{9}$
20. $\tfrac{1}{24}$
21. $\tfrac{3}{10}$
22. $\tfrac{1}{10}$
23. $\tfrac{1}{18}$
24. $\tfrac{5}{36}$
25. $\tfrac{13}{45}$

Page 33
1. $\tfrac{12}{49}$
2. $\tfrac{3}{10}$
3. $\tfrac{10}{27}$
4. $\tfrac{5}{24}$
5. $\tfrac{1}{2}$
6. $\tfrac{1}{12}$
7. $\tfrac{7}{27}$
8. $\tfrac{7}{25}$
9. $\tfrac{1}{2}$
10. $\tfrac{9}{44}$
11. $\tfrac{7}{10}$
12. $\tfrac{3}{10}$
13. $\tfrac{7}{33}$
14. $\tfrac{1}{4}$
15. $\tfrac{9}{11}$
16. $\tfrac{9}{16}$
17. $\tfrac{21}{32}$
18. $\tfrac{27}{70}$
19. $\tfrac{3}{10}$
20. $\tfrac{1}{15}$
21. $\tfrac{9}{25}$
22. $\tfrac{3}{8}$
23. $\tfrac{3}{10}$
24. $\tfrac{6}{25}$
25. $\tfrac{4}{35}$

Page 34
1. $1\tfrac{1}{3}$
2. $1\tfrac{1}{4}$
3. $2\tfrac{1}{42}$
4. $1\tfrac{23}{28}$
5. $1\tfrac{1}{3}$
6. $1\tfrac{13}{33}$
7. $1\tfrac{2}{3}$
8. $1\tfrac{5}{34}$
9. 1
10. $1\tfrac{3}{5}$
11. $\tfrac{2}{3}$
12. $1\tfrac{13}{92}$
13. $1\tfrac{1}{3}$
14. $3\tfrac{21}{25}$
15. $1\tfrac{1}{5}$
16. $\tfrac{46}{95}$
17. $\tfrac{4}{35}$
18. $1\tfrac{17}{40}$
19. $2\tfrac{1}{4}$
20. $1\tfrac{25}{26}$
21. $2\tfrac{19}{40}$
22. $\tfrac{24}{35}$
23. $\tfrac{42}{65}$
24. $4\tfrac{7}{8}$
25. $\tfrac{3}{4}$

Page 35
1. $2\tfrac{5}{6}$
2. $15\tfrac{5}{12}$
3. $16\tfrac{3}{5}$
4. 7
5. 5
6. $8\tfrac{2}{3}$
7. $6\tfrac{5}{24}$
8. $7\tfrac{1}{6}$
9. $8\tfrac{3}{7}$
10. $7\tfrac{7}{12}$
11. $2\tfrac{9}{10}$
12. $6\tfrac{13}{40}$
13. $6\tfrac{7}{8}$
14. $12\tfrac{1}{2}$
15. $11\tfrac{4}{33}$
16. $7\tfrac{13}{20}$
17. $14\tfrac{59}{99}$
18. $2\tfrac{11}{14}$
19. $14\tfrac{1}{4}$
20. $17\tfrac{17}{21}$
21. $4\tfrac{5}{6}$
22. $4\tfrac{5}{12}$
23. $6\tfrac{3}{5}$
24. $3\tfrac{31}{35}$
25. $5\tfrac{7}{12}$

Page 36
1. 3
2. $1\tfrac{1}{3}$
3. $\tfrac{2}{3}$
4. $\tfrac{1}{7}$
5. $\tfrac{5}{12}$
6. $2\tfrac{7}{12}$
7. $\tfrac{17}{24}$
8. $2\tfrac{2}{3}$
9. $1\tfrac{1}{2}$
10. $7\tfrac{3}{4}$
11. $2\tfrac{1}{2}$
12. $\tfrac{1}{2}$
13. 3
14. $\tfrac{19}{24}$
15. $1\tfrac{1}{6}$
16. $1\tfrac{9}{35}$
17. $\tfrac{1}{24}$
18. $\tfrac{3}{4}$
19. $\tfrac{5}{6}$
20. $\tfrac{1}{2}$
21. $2\tfrac{7}{8}$
22. $\tfrac{5}{14}$
23. $2\tfrac{2}{35}$
24. $\tfrac{1}{6}$
25. $\tfrac{13}{15}$

Page 37
1. $8\tfrac{5}{16}$
2. $3\tfrac{5}{9}$
3. $12\tfrac{2}{9}$
4. $9\tfrac{9}{49}$
5. $5\tfrac{23}{24}$
6. $7\tfrac{1}{12}$
7. $4\tfrac{5}{16}$
8. $11\tfrac{17}{21}$
9. $8\tfrac{4}{9}$
10. $8\tfrac{15}{64}$
11. $11\tfrac{11}{16}$
12. $15\tfrac{15}{16}$
13. $10\tfrac{14}{25}$
14. $7\tfrac{7}{16}$
15. $4\tfrac{2}{3}$
16. $9\tfrac{3}{7}$
17. $3\tfrac{7}{16}$
18. $3\tfrac{3}{8}$
19. $9\tfrac{1}{3}$
20. $12\tfrac{15}{16}$
21. $1\tfrac{3}{5}$
22. $1\tfrac{29}{48}$
23. $8\tfrac{1}{8}$
24. $8\tfrac{1}{3}$
25. $13\tfrac{1}{15}$

Page 38
1. $1\tfrac{7}{9}$
2. $2\tfrac{11}{32}$
3. $2\tfrac{2}{9}$
4. $1\tfrac{7}{8}$
5. $1\tfrac{13}{27}$
6. $1\tfrac{1}{3}$
7. $1\tfrac{19}{36}$
8. $1\tfrac{1}{2}$
9. $1\tfrac{2}{3}$
10. $1\tfrac{13}{25}$
11. $1\tfrac{13}{28}$
12. $1\tfrac{1}{20}$
13. $1\tfrac{1}{3}$
14. $1\tfrac{1}{5}$
15. $1\tfrac{11}{35}$
16. $\tfrac{4}{5}$
17. $\tfrac{24}{35}$
18. $1\tfrac{17}{55}$
19. $2\tfrac{25}{28}$
20. $1\tfrac{101}{144}$
21. $1\tfrac{1}{6}$
22. $\tfrac{39}{50}$
23. $1\tfrac{16}{47}$
24. $1\tfrac{4}{35}$
25. $\tfrac{17}{30}$

ANSWERS

Page 39

1. 5
2. 10
3. 20
4. 40
5. 60
6. 8
7. 3
8. 45
9. 60
10. 30
11. 60
12. 10
13. 200
14. 250
15. 100
16. 75
17. 250
18. 46
19. 306
20. 8.5
21. 110
22. 70
23. 225
24. 96
25. 328

Page 40

1. 55
2. 110
3. 88
4. 132
5. 60
6. 84
7. 108
8. 144
9. 250
10. 62.5
11. 1250
12. 200
13. 195
14. 260
15. 520
16. 375
17. 450
18. 18
19. 200
20. 600
21. 375
22. 750
23. 1750
24. 1100
25. 2750

Page 41

1. 18
2. 45
3. 72
4. 170
5. 85
6. 127.5
7. 16
8. 40
9. 400
10. 21
11. 7
12. 84
13. 105
14. 1050
15. 120
16. 180
17. 48
18. 5
19. 65
20. 95
21. 32
22. 30
23. 25
24. 180
25. 850

Page 42

1. 25%
2. 5%
3. 20%
4. 15%
5. 20%
6. 80%
7. 20%
8. 0.4%
9. 10%
10. 2.5%
11. 50%
12. 20%
13. 400%
14. 40%
15. 0.5%
16. 2.5%
17. 50%
18. 0.3%
19. 5%
20. 100%
21. 10%
22. 0.25%
23. 5%
24. 0.05%
25. 0.05%

Page 44

1. 30%
2. 50%
3. 150%
4. 33.3%
5. 100%
6. 200%
7. 20%
8. 50%
9. 75%
10. 150%
11. 10%
12. 20%
13. 20%
14. 25%
15. 20%
16. 60%
17. 50%
18. 200%

Page 46

1. 15.27
2. 15.573
3. 3.71
4. 5.985
5. 225.7
6. 65.304
7. 9.69
8. 32.114
9. 5.63
10. 124.1
11. 7.022
12. 19.84
13. 12.121
14. 31.0101
15. 36.42
16. 21.81
17. 27.352
18. 7.183
19. 48.75
20. 1.1854
21. 17.7
22. 25.435
23. 103.29
24. 3.814
25. 912.939

Page 47

1. 3.22
2. 49.6
3. 3.68
4. 809.2
5. 5.413
6. 6.485
7. 0.9
8. 5.69
9. 4.07
10. 15.87
11. 2.42
12. 8.69
13. 20.76
14. 0.567
15. 1.93
16. 8.634
17. 8.45
18. 5.6
19. 1.76
20. 1.5
21. 14.1
22. 7.01
23. 15.03
24. 7.001
25. 192.32

Page 48

1. 13.2
2. 7.5
3. 4.2
4. 2.8
5. 1.5
6. 26
7. 1.2
8. 3.5
9. 1
10. 4.5
11. 2.8
12. 6.6
13. 3.6
14. 8
15. 4
16. 4.8
17. 5.6
18. 0.7
19. 3
20. 2.4
21. 7.2
22. 8.4
23. 1.2
24. 0.84
25. 0.012

Page 49

1. 40
2. 0.6
3. 500
4. 0.7
5. 50
6. 0.032
7. 1000
8. 1.1
9. 80
10. 3
11. 0.12
12. 13
13. 0.35
14. 50
15. 0.09
16. 400
17. 0.6
18. 1000
19. 50
20. 30
21. 1.2
22. 1.1
23. 400
24. 11
25. 11.1

Page 50

1. 1.2
2. 1.36
3. 2.35
4. 2.43
5. 3.123
6. 4.877
7. 15.1
8. 15.23
9. 14.456
10. 0.0006
11. 0.2
12. 0.002
13. 1.9
14. 12.23
15. 134.567
16. 12.0
17. 13.35
18. 14.232
19. 1.65
20. 1.03
21. 1.010
22. 10.03
23. 9.5
24. 10.06
25. 7.6

ANSWERS

Page 51

1. 120
2. 100
3. 4000
4. 4600
5. 57900
6. 65000
7. 766000
8. 2.35
9. 43.2
10. 1.3
11. 2.35
12. 0.0002
13. 0.0057
14. 0.00346
15. 0.0066
16. 1.00
17. 1.004
18. 120
19. 45000
20. 56000
21. 30000
22. 47000
23. 5680
24. 66000
25. 1234700

Page 52

1. 2×10^2
2. 3×10^3
3. 4×10^4
4. 5×10^5
5. 2.3×10^2
6. 2.345×10^3
7. 3.4678×10^4
8. 5.43211×10^5
9. 3.21×10^4
10. 4.32×10^3
11. 5×10^1
12. 2×10^6
13. 2×10^{-1}
14. 3×10^{-2}
15. 4×10^{-3}
16. 5×10^{-4}
17. 6×10^{-5}
18. 1.2×10^{-1}
19. 2.34×10^{-1}
20. 4.567×10^{-1}
21. 3.45×10^{-3}
22. 2.367×10^{-2}
23. 5.68×10^{-4}
24. 6.1×10^{-2}
25. 5.0063×10^{-1}

Page 53

1. 14
2. 17
3. 48
4. -2
5. 2
6. 2
7. 3
8. 51
9. 52
10. 67
11. 39
12. 33
13. 28
14. 67
15. 85
16. 39
17. 40
18. 25
19. 10
20. 90
21. 0
22. 720
23. 3
24. 27
25. 14

Page 54

1. 14
2. 10
3. 14
4. 43
5. 40
6. 13
7. 875
8. 56
9. 13
10. 48
11. 403
12. 146
13. 85
14. 37
15. 60
16. 4
17. 382
18. 28
19. 30
20. 137
21. 808
22. 23
23. 36000
24. 20
25. -36

Page 55

1. -1
2. -1
3. -2
4. 3
5. -11
6. -16
7. -11
8. 2
9. -11
10. -20
11. -10
12. -11
13. 21
14. -5
15. 0
16. -6
17. -4
18. 26
19. -5
20. 0
21. -8
22. 5
23. 2
24. -22
25. -31

Page 56

1. 13
2. 4
3. -3
4. 15
5. 10
6. 20
7. 2
8. 24
9. 75
10. -63
11. 15
12. -1
13. 41
14. 20
15. 40
16. 111
17. 26
18. 9
19. 17
20. 104
21. 18
22. 18
23. 11
24. 100
25. 20

Page 57

1. -15
2. -24
3. -30
4. 25
5. -35
6. 32
7. -22
8. -66
9. 121
10. 144
11. -5
12. 4
13. 2
14. 2
15. -5
16. 5
17. -1
18. -12
19. -11
20. 11
21. 1
22. -11
23. 11
24. 66
25. 0.5

Page 58

1. 6t + 8
2. 13a + 3b + 4ab
3. 7t - 11
4. 8s + 6t
5. 8a + 5b
6. 9m + 3n
7. 7z + y
8. 11a - 5b
9. 4a - 5b
10. 2a - 2b + 7ab
11. 6ab - 5b
12. 2y - 7f + 2fy
13. 7v + 5
14. $11q - 2q^2$
15. 0
16. 10u
17. 0
18. 3ab
19. 14pq + 3q - 5p
20. 6jh
21. 2p - 4t
22. 0
23. 10pq - 6p + 5q
24. -3jh
25. 2t - 6p

Page 59

1. 7x + 14
2. 9x − 27
3. 14x + 28
4. -3x + 9
5. -9x − 54
6. 10x + 40
7. -25x − 100
8. 7x + 7
9. -3x + 6
10. 7x + 77
11. -2x − 32
12. 3x + 126
13. -2x − 8
14. -4x + 12
15. -9x − 225
16. 7x + 140
17. 7x + 42
18. -3x − 9
19. -2x − 14
20. -4x − 20
21. -5x − 45
22. -3x + 15
23. -2x + 20
24. -3x + 15
25. -5x − 30

Page 60

1. 15
2. 11
3. 8
4. 5
5. 9
6. 3
7. 10
8. 11
9. 4
10. 4
11. 9
12. 5
13. 5
14. 8
15. 2
16. 12
17. -12
18. -9
19. -5
20. -9
21. -2
22. -8
23. -7
24. 8
25. -30

ANSWERS

Page 61

1. 250
2. 50
3. 100
4. 400
5. 100
6. 16
7. 56
8. 50
9. 15
10. 20
11. 12
12. 45
13. 500
14. 240
15. 20
16. 15
17. 500
18. 10000
19. 28
20. 400
21. 420
22. 18
23. 10
24. 4000
25. 1000000

Page 62

1. 4
2. 8
3. 8
4. 35
5. 10
6. 18
7. 5
8. 3
9. 4
10. 14
11. 9
12. 30
13. 13
14. 0
15. -14
16. 31
17. -3
18. -32
19. -1
20. 10
21. -32
22. 2
23. 30
24. -2
25. 68

Page 63

1. 15
2. 15
3. 16
4. 82
5. 15
6. 35
7. 31
8. 10
9. 35
10. 16
11. 32
12. 16
13. 15
14. 14
15. 30
16. 37
17. 35
18. 34
19. 62
20. 81
21. 36
22. 29
23. 34
24. 58
25. 111

Page 64

1. 2
2. 7
3. 6
4. 4
5. 4
6. -16
7. 20
8. 2
9. 0.5
10. 3
11. 1
12. 9
13. 2
14. 1.5
15. 1
16. 0.25
17. 2
18. 2
19. 2
20. 4
21. 20
22. 3
23. ⅓
24. -1
25. 5

Page 65

1. -5
2. -14
3. -6
4. -6
5. -5
6. -4
7. -4
8. -11
9. -7
10. -14
11. -7
12. -3
13. -6
14. -20
15. -5
16. -24
17. -25
18. -3
19. -1
20. -2
21. -10
22. -1
23. -3
24. -4
25. -30

Page 66

1. 4
2. 4
3. 2
4. 25
5. 2
6. 2
7. 20
8. 25
9. 2
10. 50
11. 5
12. 20
13. 10
14. 11
15. 10
16. 7.5
17. 4
18. -10
19. -40
20. 400
21. 20
22. 10
23. -95
24. 300
25. 30

Page 67

1. -5
2. -45
3. -10
4. -6
5. -2.25
6. -10
7. -3
8. -3
9. -1
10. -3
11. 1
12. -58
13. -4
14. -25
15. 30
16. -18
17. -42
18. -18
19. -7.5
20. -13
21. -50
22. -100
23. -80
24. -10
25. -19

Page 68

1. -7.5
2. -90
3. -15
4. -7.5
5. -3
6. -14
7. -4
8. -6
9. -1.5
10. -6
11. 5
12. -38
13. -6
14. -33
15. 90
16. -15
17. -63
18. -9
19. -15
20. -39
21. -14
22. 6
23. 3
24. 17
25. 5

Page 69

1. a=1 b=2
2. a=2 b=1
3. a=2 b=3
4. a=3 b=1
5. a=4 b=2
6. a=5 b=2
7. a=8 b=4
8. a=10 b=5
9. a=2 b=-2
10. a=6 b=-3
11. a=3 b=4
12. a=5 b=6
13. a=8 b=10
14. a=3 b=6
15. a=5 b=10
16. a=10 b=20
17. a=10 b=20
18. a=-1 b=2

Page 70

1. L=10cm W=5cm A=50cm²
2. H=7cm
3. L=9cm W=3cm P=24cm
4. L=2cm W=8cm P=20cm
5. H=10cm B=5cm
6. 7cm 21cm
7. B=10cm H= 20cm
8. H=12cm
9. 2cm 20cm
10. L=3cm W=6cm A=18cm²
11. B=6cm H=12cm
12. B=4cm H=16cm
13. L=4cm W=12cm P=32cm
14. L=3cm W=33cm P=72cm

ANSWERS

Page 72

1. A=25cm² P=20cm
2. A=10cm² P=16cm
3. A=49cm² P=28cm
4. A=56cm² P=32cm
5. A=77cm² P=36cm
6. A=81cm² P=36cm
7. A=45cm² P=23cm
8. A=144cm² P=48cm
9. A=96cm² P=44cm
10. A=90cm² P=37cm
11. A=44cm² P=32cm
12. A=172cm² P = 61cm
13. A=169cm² P=52cm
14. A=25cm² P=22cm
15. A=44cm² P=26cm
16. A=180cm² P=58cm
17. A=30.25cm² P=22cm
18. A=190cm² P=60cm
19. A=420cm² P=88cm
20. A=36cm² P=22cm
21. 1156cm² P=136cm
22. A=289cm² P=68cm
23. A=135cm² P=52cm

Page 74

1. 69cm²
2. 68cm²
3. 18cm²
4. 170cm²
5. 60cm²
6. 45cm²
7. 60cm²
8. 62cm²
9. 88cm²

Page 75

1. A=432cm² C=72cm
2. A=27m² C=18m
3. A=243mm² C=54 mm
4. A=1200mm² C=120 mm
5. A=147cm² C=42cm
6. A=150mm² C=50 mm
7. A=24m² C=20m
8. A=54cm² C=30cm
9. A=726cm² C=110 cm
10. A=384mm² C=80mm

Page 76

1. SA=206cm² V=165cm³
2. SA=696mm² V=880mm³
3. SA=378mm² V=360mm³
4. SA=2200cm² V=6000cm³
5. SA=454cm² V=560cm³
6. SA=910cm² V=750cm³
7. SA=4000mm² V=12500mm³
8. SA=726cm² V=1170cm³
9. SA=312cm² V=224cm³
10. SA=226mm² V=90mm³
11. SA=9600mm² V=54000mm³
12. SA=1498cm² V=2940cm³
13. SA=46000cm² V=600000cm³

Page 77

1. 324cm³
2. 120cm³
3. 1050cm³
4. 432cm³
5. 60cm³
6. 180cm³
7. 375cm³
8. 594 cm³
9. 1944cm³
10. 9000cm³
11. 528cm³
12. 204cm³
13. 69cm³

Page 78

1. 45°
2. 57°
3. 161°
4. 58°
5. 136°
6. 143°
7. 51°
8. 163°
9. 33°
10. 72°
11. 145°
12. 88°
13. 119°
14. 83°
15. 44°
16. 111°

Page 80

1. I=90° E=90°
2. I=135° E=45°
3. I=120° E=60°
4. I=60° E=120°
5. I=90° E=90°
6. I=129° E=51°
7. I=108° E=72°

Page 81

1. A=6 B=8 C=12
2. A=6 B=8 C=12
3. A=3 B=0 C=2
4. A=1 B=0 C=0
5. A=2 B=1 C=1
6. A=2 B=0 C=1
7. A=5 B=5 C=8
8. A=4 B=4 C=6
9. A=8 B=6 C=12
10. A=5 B=6 C=9
11. A=8 B=12 C=18
12. A=10 B=16 C=24

Page 82

1. $\frac{1}{4}$
2. $\frac{3}{10}$
3. $\frac{7}{20}$
4. $\frac{1}{10}$
5. $\frac{13}{20}$
6. $\frac{7}{10}$
7. $\frac{3}{5}$
8. $\frac{3}{10}$
9. $\frac{3}{100}$
10. $\frac{9}{80}$
11. $\frac{39}{200}$
12. $\frac{1}{38}$
13. $\frac{27}{190}$
14. $\frac{14}{95}$
15. $\frac{1}{16}$
16. $\frac{1}{190}$
17. 0

Page 84

1. $\frac{1}{2}$
2. $\frac{1}{2}$
3. $\frac{1}{2}$
4. $\frac{1}{6}$
5. $\frac{1}{3}$
6. $\frac{2}{3}$
7. $\frac{1}{6}$
8. $\frac{1}{36}$
9. $\frac{1}{216}$
10. $\frac{1}{4}$
11. 1
12. $\frac{1}{27}$
13. 0
14. 0
15. $\frac{1}{12}$
16. $\frac{1}{6}$
17. $\frac{1}{6}$

Page 86

1. $\frac{1}{2}$
2. $\frac{1}{2}$
3. $\frac{1}{4}$
4. $\frac{1}{4}$
5. $\frac{4}{13}$
6. $\frac{5}{13}$
7. $\frac{4}{13}$
8. $\frac{2}{13}$
9. $\frac{1}{13}$
10. $\frac{1}{13}$
11. $\frac{9}{13}$
12. $\frac{1}{169}$
13. $\frac{1}{26}$
14. $\frac{1}{338}$
15. $\frac{4}{663}$
16. $\frac{1}{102}$
17. $\frac{1}{4}$
18. $\frac{1}{676}$

ANSWERS

Page 88

1. 28
2. 25
3. 38
4. 25
5. 26
6. -19
7. 81
8. 309
9. 0.5
10. 9
11. 155
12. 151
13. 37
14. 16
15. -127
16. 20.5
17. 320
18. -1287

Page 90

1a. 5000mm
1b. 500cm
2a. 100m
2b. 0.1km
3a. 70000mm
3b. 7000cm
4a. 120m
4b. 0.12km
5a. 800m
5b. 0.8km
6a. 490m
6b. 0.49km
7a. 1200m
7b. 1.2km
8a. 300m
8b. 0.3km
9a. 20000m
9b. 20km
10a. 18000m
10b. 18km
11a. 80000m
11b. 80km
12a. 1000000m
12b. 1000km
13a. 24m
13b. 0.024km
14a. 4000000m
14b. 4000km
15a. 300000m
15b. 300km
16. 1500000m
16b. 1500km
17a. 2500000m
17b. 2500km
18a. 10000000m
18b. 10000km

Page 92

1. 60cm
2. 45cm
3. 40cm
4. 50cm
5. 200cm
6. 50cm
7. 5cm
8. 1000cm
9. 5cm
10. 20mm
11. 5mm
12. 400cm
13. 50000cm
14. 200cm
15. 50cm
16. 6.3cm
17. 0.95cm
18. 0.4cm

Page 94

1. 0.7km
2. 80000g
3. 340ml
4. 2600g
5. 500mm
6. 40000mg
7. 0.31km
8. 908cl
9. 0.7 tonnes
10. 6.55km
11. 7.86l
12. 2300000mg
13. 3100cl
14. 0.2202km
15. 70kg
16. 450cl
17. 207.6cm
18. 300000cm
19. 3000mm
20. 5000ml
21. 20cm
22. 3500000cm
23. 30000mm
24. 15000ml
25. 6kg

Page 96

1. 39ft
2. 63lbs
3. 6720lbs
4. 960 inches
5. 80 ounces
6. 2400 pints
7. 88 yards
8. 1123 yards
9. 15 stone
10. 2 tonnes
11. 12ft
12. 100lbs
13. 70 gallons
14. 5 miles
15. 0.0003ft
16. 98lbs
17. 0.112lbs
18. 36 inches
19. 1120 ounces
20. 40 pints
21. 90ft
22. 91 pounds
23. 11200 pounds
24. 14400 inches
25. 256 ounces

Page 98

1. £10
2. 0.55 Euros
3. $2.50
4. 1 200 Francs
5. 402 Yen
6. 11 Euros
7. $25
8. 0.3 Francs
9. 4 020 Yen
10. 11000 Euros
11. 160800 Yen
12. £0.01
13. 0.6 Francs
14. £40.00
15. $6.25
16. £20
17. £100
18. £2000
19. £2000
20. $1250
21. 1.34 Yen
22. £80
23. £100
24. $12000
25. 26.8 Yen

Page 100

1. 100
2. 150
3. 30
4. 2.5
5. 1.5
6. 36
7. 0.3
8. 14
9. 0.8
10. 200
11. 140
12. 2
13. 2
14. 60
15. 40
16. 60
17. 4
18. 800
19. 20
20. 2
21. 100
22. 70
23. 5
24. 100
25. 800

Page 101

1. 15
2. 25
3. 10000
4. 16
5. 38
6. 140
7. 33
8. 8
9. 63
10. -6
11. 84
12. 4
13. 200
14. 5.8
15. 45
16. 10
17. 13
18. 36
19. 125
20. 21
21. 37
22. 50
23. 105
24. 126
25. 1700

Page 102

1. 7n + 1
2. 10n + 46
3. 120 − 20n
4. 8n + 5
5. 3n + 15
6. n²
7. 10n + 10
8. 82 − 12n
9. n − 0.5
10. 14 − 5n
11. 50n − 46
12. 2n + 9
13. 33n − 33
14. 67 − 11n
15. 75 − 15n
16. -4n
17. 2n + 1
18. 3n + 1
19. n3
20. 10n + 5
21. 20n + 10
22. 3n − 2
23. 5n + 4
24. 30n − 24
25. 400n − 300

ANSWERS

Page 104

1. 5:37pm	10. 23:53	19. 02:44
2. 3:20am	11. 12:18	20. 08:59
3. 1:10am	12. 07:36	21. 15:28
4. 7:55pm	13. 21:09	22. 07:59
5. 1:46pm	14. 13:42	23. 07:52
6. 12:00am	15. 18:00	24. 18:59
7. 9:09am	16. 03:44	25. 11:59
8. 6:14pm	17. 05:59	
9. 12:00pm	18. 16:28	

Page 106

1. 7h28	10. 31h24	19. 16h51
2. 55h20	11. 4h37	20. 6h10
3. 6h33	12. 80h51	21. 0h3
4. 39h24	13. 4h47	22. 3h43
5. 5h6	14. 48h	23. 2h51
6. 49h9	15. 16h56	24. 9h36
7. 9h50	16. 73h5	25. 64h1
8. 50h25	17. 5h18	
9. 2h20	18. 44h30	

Page 108

1. 135°	7. 75°	13. 130°
2. 10°	8. 45°	14. 180°
3. 0°	9. 90°	15. 30°
4. 120°	10. 20°	16. 150°
5. 60°	11. 10°	17. 15°
6. 70°	12. 15°	18. 90°

Page 110

1. (-5 4) (-1 4) (-3 7)
2. (3 2) (3 4) (8 2) (8 4)
3. (-10 -5) (-8 -5) (-9 -7)
4. (5 0) (5 -2) (10 0) (10 -2)
5. (5 4) (1 4) (3 7)
6. (-2 4)
7. (8 2) (4 2) (6 5)
8. Reflect in the y-axis and translate by (0 3)
9. (5 -6) (3 -6) (4 -8)
10. (1 6) (1 8) (6 6) (6 8)

Page 112

1a. 46	18. 1/16
1b. 42	19. 140 miles
2a. 36	19b. 210 min
2b 26	19c. London
3a. 30	20. £100
3b. 60	21. £500
4. 49	22. 55
5. 12	23. 5050
6. 57	24. 500500
7. 36	25a. 1234700
8. 600	25b. 123.47
9. 99	25c. 1500
10. Same	25d. 15
11. 50	26a. £1100
12. 70	26b. £1210
13. £220	26c. £1331
14. £11	27. 2x2x2x2x3
15. 5	28. 2x2x3x3
16. 3	29. 1200
17. 1/12	30. 2025

Page 115

1. 30	4. 7/20	7. 54
2. 33	5. 6	
3. 100	6. 4	

Page 116

1. 20	4. 30	7. ¾
2. ⅛	5. 50%	
3. 70	6. 30	

Page 117

1. ⅔	4. 75	7. 30
2. 15	5. ⅙	
3. ⅓	6. 45	

Page 118

1. 08:35	9. D
2. B	10. B
3. A	11. 07:10
4. B	12. 270 min
5. 230 min	13. C
6. 150 min	14. D
7. B	15. D.
8. 08:10	

Page 120

1. 7	8. 50%
2. Barcelona	9. 18
3. Messi	10. 15
4. Rashford	11. 5:6
5. 2	12. ½
6. 4	13. Suarez
7. Rashford	

Page 122

1. 5	4. 1	7. 4
2. 4	5. 0	8. Infinite
3. 1	6. 1	

Page 123

1. 3	4. 5	7. 1
2. 4	5. 1	8. 2
3. Infinite	6. 2	

Page 124

1. 60 miles	11. 10 seconds
2. 200 miles	12. 2000 seconds
3. 120 miles	13. 8 hours
4. 200 m	14. 2.5 hours
5. 1.8 km	15. 0.67 seconds
6. 200 km/hr	16. 10 m/s
7. 100 miles/hr	16b. 8 m/s
8. 8.5 m/s	17. 420 miles
9. 0.01 m/s	17b. 315 minutes
10. 1.25 miles/hr	17c. Manchester